◆ A PADDLER'S GUIDE TO ◆

Quetico
and Beyond

• A PADDLER'S GUIDE TO •

Quetico
and Beyond

KEVIN CALLAN

The BOSTON
MILLS PRESS

A BOSTON MILLS PRESS BOOK

Copyright © 2007 Kevin Callan

Published by Boston Mills Press, 2007
132 Main Street, Erin, Ontario N0B 1T0
Tel: 519-833-2407 Fax: 519-833-2195

The publisher gratefully acknowledges the financial support for our publishing program,
from the Canada Council, the Ontario Arts Council and the Government of Canada
through the Book Publishing Industry Development Program. (BPIDP)

Library and Archives Canada Cataloguing in Publication

Callan, Kevin
A paddler's guide to Quetico and beyond / Kevin Callan.

Includes bibliographical references and index.
ISBN-13: 978-1-55046-500-6 (pbk.)
ISBN-10: 1-55046-500-7 (pbk.)

1. Canoes and canoeing — Ontario — Quetico Provincial Park Region — Guidebooks.
2. Quetico Provincial Park Region (Ont.) — Guidebooks.
I. Title. II. Title: Quetico and beyond.

GV776.15.Q86C34 2007   797.122'09713117   C2006-906839-9

Publisher Cataloging-in-Publication Data (U.S.)

Callan, Kevin.
A paddler's guide to Quetico and beyond / Kevin Callan.
[192] p. : col. photos., maps ; cm.
Includes bibliographical references and index.

Summary: Canoe routes through Quetico Provincial Park
and the surrounding area; includes 16 trips with route maps.

ISBN-10: 1-55046-500-7 (pbk.)
ISBN-13: 978-1-55046-500-6 (pbk.)

1. Canoes and canoeing – Ontario – Quetico Provincial Park Region –
Guidebooks. 2. Quetico Provincial Park Region (Ont.) – Guidebooks. I. Title.

797.122'09713 dc22 GV776.15.Q86C34 2007

Maps by Tim Wykes
Text design by Mary Firth and Gillian Stead
Cover design by Gillian Stead
Overleaf: *Payne Lake*

Printed in China

Contents

Solitude on Jesse Lake.

Acknowledgments

*For my father, who introduced me to the peace one finds fishing in
a trout stream, the glorious sound of a crackling campfire, the intrinsic
value of a remote wilderness setting, and the art of telling a good story.*

IF IT'S TRUE WHAT MY FATHER SAID, that you can judge the richness of
your life by the friends you have made along the way, then I claim a very wealthy
existence. And to have an opportunity such as this to thank some of them is very
special to me.

First, I would like to thank the friends who paddled with me: Nancy Scott, Kip
Spidell, Robin Reilly, Catherine Reilly, my wife Alana, daughter Kyla (and dog
Bailey), and especially Andy Baxter. A special note of gratitude goes out to Andy's
wife, Marion, their children Sean, Patricia and Shannon, and dog Monty for
allowing him to head off paddling with me for weeks on end.

A big thanks to Tim Wykes for producing original maps, to book designers
Mary Firth and Gill Stead, and to the gang at Boston Mills Press (Noel Hudson,
Kathy Fraser and John Denison). Thanks also to Jim Stevens at Eureka Tents and
Packs, Bill and Anne at Ostrom Packs, Glenn Fallis from Voyageur Canoes,
Randy Austin from Dunham Boots, and Keith Robinson from Souris River
Canoes, for supplying me with some great gear during this writing project.

Special credit goes to the staff at
Quetico Provincial Park, especially
Superintendent Robin Reilly and Assistant
Superintendent Dave Maynard, the Friends
of Quetico, especially Director Catherine
Reilly, and the Quetico Foundation. Their
dedication to the protection of wilderness
and wilderness values is exceptional and
their friendship to me while working on
this project is unforgettable.

Finally, I would like to thank the people who contributed to the last three chapters of this book: Lynn Cox, Scott Warner,
Kathy Warner, Phil Cotton and Barry
Simon. The work they are doing to help
preserve and promote places to canoe is
very timely and much appreciated by all
of us who paddle.

*Andy gives a special thank you to Assistant
Superintendent Dave Maynard.*

Alana and Bailey lead the way to Burke Lake.

Introduction

THE FIRST TIME I VISITED QUETICO, I stopped at the main campground for the night while on a road trip to western Canada. The park was on my list of places to see along the way, and in my journal that evening I wrote, "Lots of trees, lots of lakes, nothing really special except for a bald eagle sighting near the park gate. Not sure what all the hype is about this place."

Five years later I returned for a weeklong canoe trip in the park's interior. It was my wife's idea. My journal entry for the last night out was a little different than the one from my initial visit: "I'm in love with this place. Quetico is definitely made for the canoe, or, better yet, the canoe is perfectly made for Quetico. It truly is a paddler's paradise."

How could I have such a dissimilar view the second time around? I think it's because on my initial visit I was merely a tourist looking for some postcard image, a sightseer with a checklist. Only after my canoe trip in the interior did I actually experience what Quetico had to offer.

It's not as if this place doesn't have its share of snapshot-worthy natural wonders. There are majestic waterfalls, peaceful lakes, stands of old-growth pine, massive chunks of granite decorated with ancient pictographs, and even the odd bald eagle sighting. But Quetico is much more than that. It's calm evenings spent lying in the tent listening to the loons' call; picking marble-sized wild blueberries for morning pancakes; taking on a challenging portage to some remote lake full of feisty fish; and traveling the same rivers once used by Sioux and Ojibwe warriors and French fur-traders.

In my mind, paddling Quetico Park represents a perfect canoe trip: life becomes so simple that the stress of the "real" world is left far behind. It can be the kind of trip during which you finally begin to understand why wilderness is so important to the human soul.

That evening spent in the main campground had little meaning to me, but the weeklong canoe trip in Quetico's interior changed my life. From there I ventured to even wilder places in northwestern Ontario. I went beyond Quetico to visit places such as White Otter Castle on the Turtle River and Wendell Beckwith's "Center of the Universe" in Wabakimi. The route choices are endless.

Along the way I met many kindred spirits who feel the same way I do about this part of the country: volunteers such as Phil Cotton and Barry Simon, who spend their holidays in northern Wabakimi Provincial Park making lost canoe routes found again; canoe-trippers such as Scott and Kathy Warner, who are committed to exploring rarely used portions of Woodland Caribou Provincial Park; and outfitters such as Lynn Cox, from Canoe Frontiers, who has dedicated her life

Quetico Provincial Park

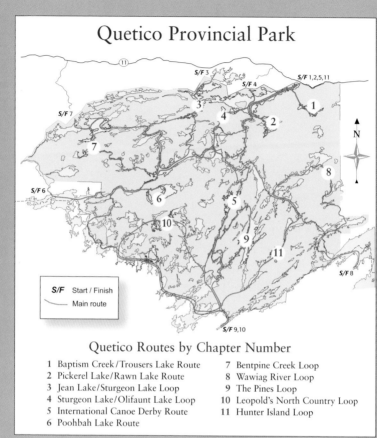

S/F   Start / Finish

Main route

Quetico Routes by Chapter Number

1 Baptism Creek/Trousers Lake Route
2 Pickerel Lake/Rawn Lake Route
3 Jean Lake/Sturgeon Lake Loop
4 Sturgeon Lake/Olifaunt Lake Loop
5 International Canoe Derby Route
6 Poohbah Lake Route

7 Bentpine Creek Loop
8 Wawiag River Loop
9 The Pines Loop
10 Leopold's North Country Loop
11 Hunter Island Loop

Beyond the Park

16 Woodland Caribou

14 Upper Albany River

13,15 Wabakimi

12 White Otter Lake

Quetico (see map above)

MANITOBA

ONTARIO

CANADA
USA

LAKE SUPERIOR

MINNESOTA

MICHIGAN

LAKE MICHIGAN

LAKE HURON

WISCONSIN

Louisa Falls is one of the most scenic cascades in Quetico.

to promoting such places as the Albany River in order to save them.

I think I matured as a canoeist after my trip in Quetico's interior. It made me eager to search out more wild places and excited to expand my family of friends who share my admiration for this incredible landscape and the deep desire to protect it for future use.

Between trips further north I returned to Quetico time and time again, not only to reminisce about my first canoe trip there, but also because there are always more lakes and rivers to explore. Many trips later, I'm still in love with this place, a piece of wilderness that remains truly a "paddler's paradise."

▶ A Note About Portage Lengths

CANADIAN CANOEISTS generally measure the length of a portage in meters. However, the use of rods (16.5 feet or 5.5 m or, better yet, the length of an average canoe) is a very traditional measurement for American canoeists using Quetico. The description for each route has the portage distances in rods, yards and meters.

QUETICO

Robin and Catherine Reilly search for water on not-so-navigable Baptism Creek.

1 Baptism Creek/Trousers Lake Route

THERE'S DEFINITELY AN ADVANTAGE in Quetico's main campground being situated on French and Pickerel Lakes. It makes an incredible amount of water easily accessible, which is perfect if you're a novice paddler or camper who has limited time for a trip. The down side is that the lakes are so big that it's too darn windy most of the time to get anywhere. That's where Trousers Lake comes in.

To me this route beats battling waves out on French and Pickerel Lakes hands down. The trip consists of small creek and lake paddling, where wind is usually not an issue. It's also not that busy. I'm not sure why. Maybe because Baptism Creek, leading to Trousers Lake, is the waterway used to link up with the Cache Lake route — a nightmare of a trip that has the longest and muddiest portages in all of Quetico, measuring close to three miles (about 5 km). If you do meet up with someone en route they are usually on their way to the first carry to Cache and aren't thinking about staying on a lake so "civilized" as Trousers. I've been to Cache, however, and Trousers Lake is pretty similar, and the trip there is certainly less painful.

One of the biggest challenges of this route is making sure you head up the right waterway. Baptism Creek is the first to enter French Lake and is located along the south shore, not far from the canoe launch area. The problem is that most paddlers will be taking the second outlet along the south shore, as the Pickerel River joins French Lake with Pickerel Lake. Just make sure not to follow the wrong crowd.

You'll get a second chance to make a wrong turn when, less then an hour's paddle upstream, the creek forks. The French River comes in from the left and Baptism Creek continues to the right. Go to the right.

From here the route is a half-day's paddle up a twisting creek, usually blocked by the odd beaver dam and/or log pile that may or may not have to be carried over, depending on water levels. If the water levels are extremely low, I suggest you consider giving up on your trip altogether. The route is navigable most of the time, but in late summer Baptism Creek has been known to dry up enough to turn a moderate route into a very difficult slog.

There are also four portages and a few swifts to negotiate. The first is a simple 40-rod (220 yd/200 m) carry to the right of shallow rapid. The only problem you might encounter on this trail, and others in the Quetico region, is that since the route is rarely used, the pathway may be blocked by a few downed trees. The second portage (85 rods/468 yd/425 m), also marked on the right, is longer and runs straight through a swampy section that can be a pain after a heavy rain. The third, found on the left, is 44 rods (242 yd/220 m) and runs alongside a stunted

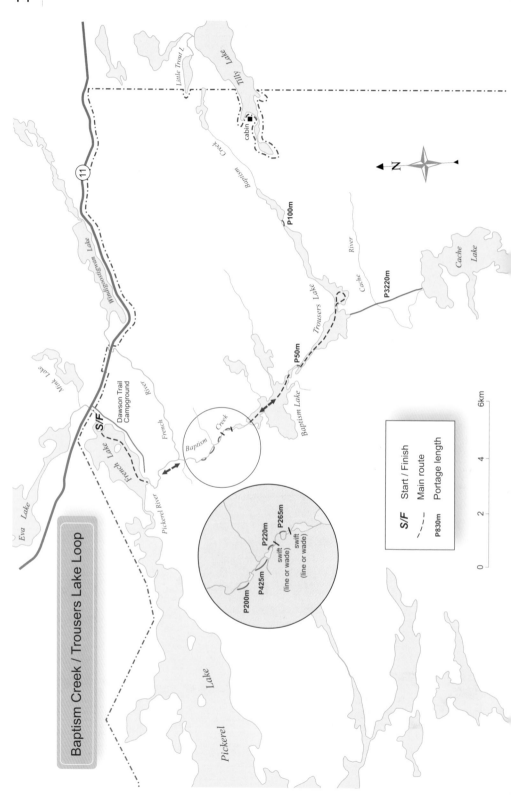

Baptism Creek / Trousers Lake Loop

Little Trout L.

Tilly Lake

cabin

Baptism Creek

11

P100m

Cache River

Trousers Lake

P3220m

Cache Lake

Windigoostigwan Lake

P50m

Baptism Lake

Mink Lake

Dawson Trail Campground

S/F

French River

French Lake

Eva Lake

Baptism Creek

P200m
P425m
P220m
P265m
swift
(line or wade)
swift
(line or wade)

Pickerel River

Pickerel Lake

S/F   Start / Finish
- - - -   Main route
P830m   Portage length

N

0   2   4   6km

cascade, with an extended takeout during high water. The fourth (53 rods/292 yd/265 m) is also on the left, has an alternative takeout, and goes up a moderate slope, ending abruptly at a slab of rock that you're forced to scramble down. A section of swift water must be waded or lined up between the third and fourth portage, and two additional swifts must be dealt with where the creek flushes out of Baptism Lake.

Baptism Lake is quite scenic, but Trousers Lake is even more so and has far better campsites to choose from. To get there you only need to take a 10-rod (55 yd/50 m) portage located at the southeast bay of Baptism.

The one dreaded portage leading to Cache Lake is located at the southeast end of the lake. Trousers continues to the left, linked by way of three separate channels. All the choice campsites are on the initial portion of Trousers Lake, but what remains to the east makes for an excellent side trip if you want to view moose or catch trophy-size pike. Only the third channel needs to be portaged (approximately 20 rods/110 yd/100 m to the right). However, from there the route quickly becomes unmanageable. Trust me on this one. A year ago the superintendent of the park, Robin Reilly, and I traveled from Tilly to Trousers in an attempt to retrace a route thought to have been taken by legendary park ranger Art Madsen. We knew Madsen had trekked back and forth to the French Lake headquarters from his Tilly Lake cabin (built in 1936). The question remained, however, whether he did this by canoe or by snowshoe. If indeed it was by canoe, then

Robin and Catherine Reilly at Tilly Lake Cabin.

Robin could plan construction of another quick-and-easy one-night outing for paddlers at the campground.

Robin partnered with his wife, Catherine (who also represents the Friends of Quetico), and I joined my frequent canoe partner Andy Baxter. It was only an overnighter for Robin and Catherine, but we were to continue on for another 20 days of paddling in the park, which of course made our gear slightly heavier than theirs. This wasn't a concern at the time, since we had checked the map and — believing that the upper segment of Baptism Creek was navigable — we guessed we would have only 120 rods (660 yd/600 m) of bushwhacking from the south-west end of Tilly.

Everything started off as planned. There was a good road leading off Highway 11 to the creek separating Tilly Lake and Laughren Lake, then only a liftover and an easy 30-rod (165 yd/150 m) portage to the right of the creek to reach Tilly Lake. After camping on a gorgeous beach on the north shore of Tilly — where Keith Robinson, the owner of Souris Canoes, surprised us by paddling in just before midnight to deliver a bottle of wine — we were up early to explore Madsen's cabin.

It was after completing a quick liftover just past the cabin, followed by 120 rods (660 yd/600 m) of bushwhacking to the creek, that the trip got interesting.

Baptism Creek was a mere trickle surrounded by an ocean of swamp grass. It was only the first week in June and water levels were still high everywhere except for in Baptism Creek.

Sweeping up mouse droppings at Tilly Lake Cabin.

Prime beach site on Tilly Lake.

Logic should have told us to turn back, but we didn't, of course. We all felt compelled to continue on, at least around the next bend, in search of a possible route. We pulled the loaded canoes across the tussocks of grass, falling over each third or fourth step. It was humid, the deer flies were horrible, and there was no potable water to be found. Five hours later, we reached Trousers Lake!

Our conclusion: Art Madsen traveled by snowshoe, not by canoe. Also, paddling to Trousers Lake and back from the main campground on French Lake is a far better one-night trip than walking in from Tilly.

Baptism Creek / Trousers Lake Route

LENGTH: 2–3 days

PORTAGES: 10

LONGEST PORTAGE: 85 rods (468 yd/425 m)

DIFFICULTY: Novice canoe-tripping skills are required.

ACCESS: Dawson Trail Ranger Station, located at the main campground in the northeast corner of the park, just south off Highway 11. It's a 130-mile (210 km) drive west of Thunder Bay and 24 miles (39 km) east of Atikokan.

ALTERNATIVE ACCESS: None

TOPOGRAPHICAL MAPS: 52-B/11

FISHER MAPS: F-30

Andy cooks up one of his favorite dishes, veggie stir-fry with extra onions, on Rawn Lake.

2 Pickerel Lake / Rawn Lake Route

QUETICO AND ITS NEIGHBORING WILDERNESS AREAS have significant bodies of water. This, of course, can be a blessing or a curse, depending on whether you are a canoeist or a kayaker. To a canoeist, lakes such as Basswood, Pickerel, Lac la Croix, White Otter and Northern Lights simply become expansive bits of water to paddle across as quickly as possible before the crowds gather or the wind and waves pick up and delay their trips into smaller and more isolated areas. But the large lakes are exactly what kayakers are looking for. Yes, it's true that most large bodies of water can be busy with boat traffic and can change quickly from calm and serene to a place where you can easily become stormbound, but seasoned kayakers know how to deal with both. Not only can a kayak handle the potential dangers of large lakes better than a canoe, but people who choose to paddle a kayak often know how to locate all those hidden coves and inlets away from all the multitudes.

Two of the best places to kayak in Quetico are Pickerel Lake and Quetico Lake. Both offer exceptional expanses of water to explore. Pickerel Lake, however, is my first choice. It provides the easiest access, the most water, some amazing sand beaches for camping, and the bonus of a unique side trip to Rawn Lake.

The trip can be started from either Stanton Bay or directly from French Lake

Kayaking may be preferable to canoeing while traveling across the expanse of Pickerel Lake.

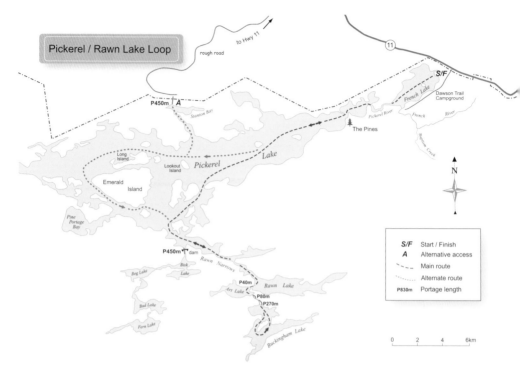

Pickerel / Rawn Lake Loop

to Hwy 11

rough road

11

S/F

French Lake

Dawson Trail
Campground

P450m | A

Stanton Bay

Pickerel River

French River

The Pines

Baptism Creek

Long
Island

Lookout
Island

Pickerel

Lake

N

Emerald
Island

Pine
Portage
Bay

P450m — dam

Rawn Narrows

Beg Lake

Bisk
Lake

P40m

Rawn Lake

Art Lake

P80m

P270m

Bud Lake

Fern Lake

Buckingham Lake

S/F	Start / Finish
A	Alternative access
- - -	Main route
....	Alternate route
P830m	Portage length

0   2   4   6km

When ya making the popcorn, Dad?
Happy camper Kyla Callan.

and the Dawson Trail campground. If you are a canoeist, Stanton Bay is the better choice as a starting point. It's more direct and has less open-water paddling. But kayakers may prefer the Dawson Trail access.

Once you've launched from the campground, keep to the left shoreline and don't mistake the entrance to Baptism Creek for that of Pickerel River. Pickerel River is the second weedy entrance, much further along the lake. Also, don't be disheartened by the crowds congregating in the Pickerel River narrows that separate French Lake and Pickerel Lake. These crowds are mostly made up of paddlers looking for a

The aftermath of the 2003 windstorm at The Pines, Pickerel Lake.

quick fix, and you'll leave them all behind once you pass the first island out on Pickerel Lake. During my last visit here, I passed a large group of over-enthusiastic anglers equipped with at least five rods each; a couple of not-so-smart teenage boys attempting to keep their banana-shaped whitewater canoe in a straight line; and an older couple sitting in lawn chairs duct-taped inside their Grumman canoe (the man in the back paddling while the woman in the front kept busy knitting a sweater). It was one of the oddest things I've even seen in all my years of canoe-tripping.

The first place to visit en route is The Pines. A 30-minute paddle beyond the entrance to Pickerel Lake, you come to a long beach, the second found along the left-hand shoreline. The backdrop to the beach area is a small patch of what remains of the old-growth red and white pine forest that drew tourists here for years. The Pines was a regular stopover for day users walking or paddling from the campground. And it still is, but a vicious windstorm struck here in the summer of 2003 and toppled hundreds of the 300-year-old trees. The pines along the shoreline somehow survived the high winds, but the surrounding hills, behind the beach, are a huge mess of fallen and uprooted trees. It's still an impressive sight, however, and worth a visit.

From The Pines you've got the entire expanse of Pickerel Lake to explore. Most paddlers head directly west, reaching Pickerel Narrows or even Batchewaung Bay in a couple of days, and then return to Dawson. But a nice side trip to Rawn Lake

Rawn Lake has a charm all to its own.

is also an option. A few hours of paddling west on Pickerel Lake, you'll reach Lookout Island. Rawn Lake, named after Superintendent Lloyd Rawn (1935-1948), is to the south and then southeast along Rawn Narrows. Island sites are available and the large cliff makes for a nice backdrop. It can still be a little busy here at times, and because of that, Rawn Lake also has a history of nuisance bears wandering into camp, so you might consider taking the easy 8-rod (44 yd/40 m) portage in from the far western bay to Art Lake, or even further to the south of Art to Buckingham by way of two portages to the left of a creek (16 and 54 rods/87 and 295 yd/80 and 270 m). Buckingham Lake is named after the chief fire ranger in 1938, and Art Lake is named after Art Madsen, one of the original 16 rangers hired in the park in 1934.

Camping over on any of these side lakes is a wonderful way to pay homage to the original park rangers. Imagine, when men like Buckingham and Madsen worked in Quetico, much of it wasn't even mapped. An average outing for them would have been further than most of us will travel in a lifetime. In one winter Madsen clocked 1,500 miles by snowshoe. He also claimed to have visited all the lakes in the park — and there are over 600 of them.

The original park rangers have been immortalized in dozens of tales written about them fighting forest fires, rescuing campers and nabbing poachers. The best characterization I've ever read is Sigurd Olson's depiction of ranger Walt Hurn:

The scraggly little pine on the end of the point belongs to memory of Walt

Hurn. It is bent and twisted, had once been flattened against the rock by some storm on the past, only to point upward again. Now it is anchored in a cleft of the greenstone, having only a few tortured branches that have survived the winds. They are gnarled and out of shape, but hold their tufts of needles defiantly against the sky. The little pine is part of Listening Point and of my memories as well. It belongs there, would be out of place in a fertile protected valley. Conditioned by the past, it can never grow tall and straight like the rest, but will always reveal its background.

Walt Hurn, once Canadian ranger at King's Point just to the north, was like that pine, for he too had weathered the storms and in the process had become just as gnarled, indestructible and indigenous.

Olson's description of Walt Hurn does justice to the tradition of Quetico's stewardship. Rangers today generally get around by motorboat and floatplane, and the park may be better protected now than it was during Hurn's day, but there was definitely a bit more romance to the job back then.

Pickerel Lake / Rawn Lake Route

LENGTH: 2–3 days

PORTAGES: 0
(3 if you take the side trip)

LONGEST PORTAGE: 0 (56 rods/
306 yds/280 m if you take the side trip)

DIFFICULTY: Novice kayak or canoe-tripping skills are required.

ACCESS: Dawson Trail Ranger Station is located at the main campground in the northeast corner of the park, just south off Highway 11. It's a 130-mile (210 km) drive west of Thunder Bay and 24 miles (39 km) east of Atikokan.

ALTERNATIVE ACCESS: Stanton Bay, located about three-quarters of the way down Pickerel Lake, is used to avoid the long paddle across French and Pickerel Lakes. Permits must first be picked up at Dawson Trail Ranger Station, then drive west on Highway 11 for 6.5 miles (10 km), a half-mile (1 km) past the intersection of Highways 11 and 633. It takes approximately 40 minutes to reach the small parking area via the rough gravel road. From here, you have to portage 90 rods (495 yd/450 m) to the lake. The portage is located just to the right of the upper right-hand corner of the parking lot. At this point, only Canadian paddlers can legally park here overnight. If you are a non-resident, you must get a Canadian outfitter to drop you off there. (I'm just as confused about this policy as you are.)

TOPOGRAPHICAL MAPS:
52-B/11, 52-B/12

FISHER MAPS: F-29, F-30

*In an attempt to enhance the paddler's wilderness experience,
campsites and portages in the interior of Quetico are not marked.*

3 Jean Lake / Sturgeon Lake Loop

MY WIFE AND I FELT OUT OF PLACE as we waited in line inside the main park office in Atikokan. The groups ahead of us, obviously regulars to Quetico, rattled off their one-week itineraries as if they were simple school outings. Alana and I, however, had never paddled the interior of the park before, and when it came our turn to pay for our permit, we stood there dumbfounded when the gate attendant asked, "So, where ya headed?"

The park staff was polite, considering that the line of canoeists behind us grew considerably while we took time to look over the provincial park map taped to the wall. We found ourselves overwhelmed by the size of it all, by the prospect of trying to plot out a route with so many tangled lakes and streams to explore. And as if we hadn't annoyed the others in line enough — a line which now reached out the front doors and down the main walkway — I took valuable time to ask what the black pins stuck in clusters on the map represented. The employee, still surprisingly calm at this point, replied, "Those are this month's nuisance bear reports. If a bear either tears open a tent or walks off with a food pack, it gets a black pin."

So, there you have it. In less then 30 seconds, Alana and I laid out our first Quetico canoe route by simply connecting a series of lakes free of black pinheads. Little did we know that we had also created an excellent introduction into the interior of the park.

We chose Nym Lake access, located on the north side of the park, as our starting point. To get there we simply had to drive east of Atikokan on Highway 11 and then turn south onto Nym Lake Road. From there it was another left onto a dirt road before the Y-intersection. The road ended at a designated parking lot, and a short trail, beginning at the southeast corner of the parking lot, led us down to the Nym Lake dock (take note that Nym Lake access point no longer has a gatehouse and that you now have to pick your permit up at the main office in Atikokan).

From the put-in, Alana and I headed south across Nym Lake, making our way through a cluster of islands and to the first portage of the trip — a 165-rod (908 yd/830 m) trail that crosses over into the park's northern boundary and leads into Batchewaung Lake.

The portage was a typical Quetico portage — mildly rolling terrain interrupted on occasion by a sharp incline or, more likely, a patch of slimy, waist-deep mud with the odd log thrown across to keep you from sinking. And in keeping with Quetico's "wilderness concept" philosophy, the takeout wasn't marked with the commonly used bright-yellow government portage sign. The location of the portage itself is shown on the park map, but none of the takeouts have signs. The same rule applies to campsites, as well. In fact, the park map doesn't even show

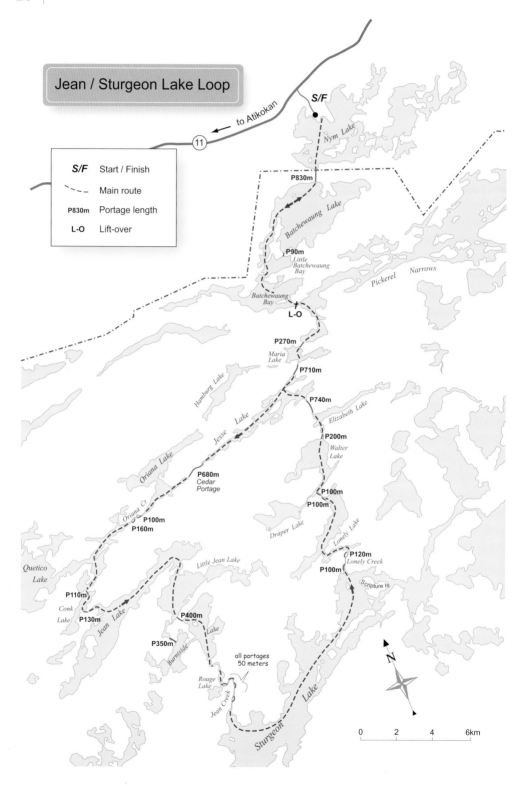

Jean / Sturgeon Lake Loop

to Atikokan
11

S/F   Start / Finish
- - - - -   Main route
P830m   Portage length
L-O   Lift-over

S/F
Nym Lake

P830m
Batchewaung Lake

P90m
Little
Batchewaung
Bay

Pickerel   Narrows

Batchewaung
Bay
L-O

P270m
Maria
Lake

P710m

Hamburg Lake

P740m
Elizabeth Lake

Jesse Lake

P200m
Walter
Lake

Oriana Lake

P680m
Cedar
Portage

P100m
P100m

Oriana Cr

Draper Lake

Lonely Lake

P100m
P160m

Little Jean Lake

P120m
Lonely Creek
P100m

Quetico
Lake

Scripture Is

P110m
Conk
Lake
P130m

Jean Lake

P400m

Lake

P350m
Burnside

all portages
50 meters

Rouge
Lake

Jean Creek

Sturgeon Lake

N

0   2   4   6km

the location of the campsites. With this in mind, however, you can stay anywhere within the boundaries of the park as long as you practice low-impact camping.

These decisions were made in the park's management plan years ago in an attempt to enhance the canoeist's wilderness experience. However, the sense of "freedom" the park has tried to create can be frustrating at times. Leaving the campsites and portages without signs, in my opinion, definitely adds to your outdoor experience, but not having the campsites marked on the map is not as beneficial. It's a good idea in theory, but most campsites have already been well established by past users, and in busier parts of Quetico you can easily become obsessed with finding an unoccupied site before darkness sets in. There are lots of non-government maps and websites that do show where the campsites are (see back of the book for details), so you can be the only paddler on the lake frantically wondering where to stop for the night if others did their homework and you didn't.

The wilderness concept originally set by the park is still a sound one. Author Sigurd Olson came to this conclusion after desperately trying to reach a particular campsite, then finding more joy in not reaching it: "With this kind of freedom, tension and strain disappear and laughter came easily."

From Batchewaung Bay our route continued on to Pickerel Narrows by way of a rock-bound channel. There is a double set of small rapids that Alana and I were able to run easily, but if the water levels had been any lower, a few jagged rocks would have been exposed and we would have considered stepping out of

"With this kind of freedom, tension and strain disappear and laughter came easily," wrote Sigurd Olson.

the canoe and either lining or wading along the left bank."

Once we entered Pickerel Narrows, we headed south past Mosquito Point and then west to the end of the isolated bay, where a 54-rod (297 yd/270 m) portage with an extremely muddy takeout led the way into Maria Lake.

This is where we spent our first night out, camping on a rocky outcrop just south of the portage. Rain had threatened all day, but we were lucky to have it hold off and turn into an incredible night sky. Wisps of clouds scudded by, unveiling clusters of stars. We decided against the tent tarp that evening and were rewarded by waking up just before midnight to view the moon shining through the canopy of jack pine that encircled us, the howl of a wolf echoing off in the distance.

The next morning a decision was made to follow the route west by portaging the 141 rods (775 yd/710 m) into Jesse Lake instead of wrestling over beaver dams along the creek flowing out of Hamburg Lake (an option some canoeists prefer).

The path beginning on the right side of the lake, where a stream trickles into the southern inlet, was unbelievably muddy despite the lack of rain. At first I attempted to jump clear of the worst spots along the trail, but after a few tumbles with the weight of the canoe crashing down on my head, I decided to take the plunge and walk straight through the muck, conceding that the being knee-deep in black ooze was simply a Quetico tradition.

Once we made it through the mud bath, Jesse Lake offered us some excellent opportunities for viewing wildlife, especially near the shallows at the east end. Just before the takeout for Cedar Portage, Alana and I were fortunate enough to spot the antics of three river otters. We spooked them, causing them to leap off the rock ledge and into the lake. The first two possessed the grace of Olympic divers. The third, however, managed to trip on a small pebble at the edge of the rock face and flopped into the lake belly-first. We couldn't help but laugh at the poor fellow as his comrades stood high in the water, their heads up like periscopes, wondering what on earth had happened to their clumsy friend.

Cedar Portage measures 135 rods (742 yd/680 m) and leads into the south bay of Oriana Lake, where you should paddle directly west to Oriana Creek and take two consecutive short portages on the left (20 rods/110 yd/100 m and 30 rods/165 yd/160 m).

The second of the two portages ends where Oriana Creek tumbles into the eastern arm of Quetico Lake. The lake itself is huge, with the main body situated to the west. To stay on route, take a quick paddle south into a large bay (look for three small islands clustered together near the entrance).

A short but relatively steep 22-rod (120 yd/110 m) portage is located near the bay's southwest corner. The takeout is to the extreme right of a 30-foot (10 m) cascade gushing out of Conk Lake. Look for the rusted debris of Quetico's logging era scattered along the shoreline at both the takeout and the put-in.

After a quick paddle across Conk Lake, another short 25-rod (138 yd/130 m)

On the way to one of Quetico's favorite stopovers, Jean Lake.

portage takes you into Jean Lake. If you're lucky, the wind will be from the west, allowing you to sail down to the sandy peninsula, a popular camping site, just ahead of the entrance to the lake's large southern bay.

Eager to take advantage of the good weather and put more distance behind us, Alana and I decided to continue across the 80-rod (440 yd/400 m) portage from Jean Lake to Burntside Lake (look for the remnants of the old ranger's cabin near the put-in). What a foolish move. After a ten-hour day, it was more than disappointing to see the first three island campsites already occupied; the first two by canoeists and the third by a marauding bear who was busy ripping open gear gathered from the site of the second group of paddlers.

We quickly moved on and it was close to 8:00 P.M. by the time we found a less-than-suitable spot on a tiny island to the south end of Burntside. Alana set up the tent in a tight spot between two pine trees, and I took time out to put another black dot on our map, adding one more nuisance bear for the park to warn campers about.

Knowing there would be a good chance of high winds and waves out on Sturgeon Lake, Alana and I woke bright and early the next day to take advantage of the morning calm; before 5:00 A.M., to be exact. At 5:30 we were packed and paddling through the narrows at Burntside's southern end, entered Rouge Lake, and then navigated Jean Creek. The creek was shallow, rocky and weedy. It also had a couple of beaver dams to lift over and four portages to carry across. The

Have tump, will travel. The author portages along Jean Creek.

portages, all found on the left, were less then 10 rods (55 yd/50 m) long. High water levels even made the fourth unnecessary; we just dodged a few half-submerged rocks and pushed our way through a patch of matted weeds. The only difficult part of the morning was trying to avoid the poison ivy growing along the portages and paddling around a large bull moose standing in midstream.

We managed to reach Sturgeon Lake by mid-morning, but in this case, the early bird didn't get the worm. As we paddled into the expanse of Sturgeon Lake, rain pelted down hard and strong winds whipped up whitecaps on every second or third trough. We tried to make the best of things by beaching the canoe in the calm of a back bay, and under a saggy tarp we cooked up a hardy brunch of camp coffee and flapjacks. While waiting for each pancake top to bubble, I would crawl out from under the tarp and watch for the slightest change in the weather. Two bowls of batter later, the pitch of wind started to die and we made the decision to head back out on the water.

The wind was blowing from the south, blasting the waves directly into our bow at first. Then, as we made our way east, hugging the north shore, the oncoming waves began lapping hard against the slide of the canoe. The rough water really didn't ease up until we reached the more protected east end of Sturgeon. And before that we were forced to head out directly across the gaping mouths of three large bays. Here I adjusted the direction of our bow in response to each wave. Most of the time the canoe would respond well, plunging through the rough parts. But there were some dicey moments, especially when I would misjudge the angle or size of the curling water and a white spray would find its way over the gunwale.

Once we navigated through the narrows at the east end of Sturgeon Lake, before Scripture Island, we pointed the bow of the canoe to the northeast, toward the portage into Lonely Creek. With the wind now directly behind us, the canoe literally surfed on top of the ruffled water. Ten minutes later we found ourselves drifting in a tranquil lagoon setting where Lonely Creek trickles into the weedy basin to the right of the portage. Alana leapt to shore the moment the bow scraped up on the pebble beach, leaving me to crawl over the packs while she raced over to the nearest tree, gave it a hug, and like a shipwrecked sailor, yelled out, "Land! Land!"

The high winds had ruined any chance of us exploring Sturgeon Lake. We were just thankful to have successfully crossed it. But our original plan was to paddle over to the elongated island southwest of Scripture Island. This place held a wood yard to fuel the steam barges that transported the first pioneers to Manitoba, initiated by Simon J. Dawson in 1857. It was also a known camping area for Sioux war parties and of voyageurs who passed through on their way west.

After Alana and I had hugged and kissed all the trees along the shore, we moved on, up Lonely Creek. Two steep portages (the first measuring 20 rods/110 yd/100 m and the second 24 rods/132 yd/120 m, both found on the left) led us

The last morning of a trip is always more special than the first (Batchewaung Bay).

into and then out of the shallow stream. Then, at the northeast end of Lonely Lake, the route followed over two more steep but short 20-rod (110 yd/100 m) portages into Walter Lake.

It was late afternoon by the time we made it to Walter, and in the distance we could hear the ominous rumble of thunder, so we made haste along the shoreline, looking for a spot to spend the night. The first possibility was a somewhat inhospitable campsite far back in a dense patch of spruce trees, but I felt that we should press on to an island farther north. We went for it, but halfway across the weather turned grey and squally, and by the time we pulled the canoe ashore, the storm was dangerously close.

First we secured the rain tarp, and then, while Alana set up the tent, I ran off into the backwoods to gather firewood, both of us feeling quite proud of the fact that we had raced against the elements and won — or so we thought! Minutes later I came running back to camp to tell Alana we were sharing the island with a bear.

With bolts of lightning crackling overhead and hard rain pelting down on the lake, the second "nuisance bear" of the trip forced us to pack our bags and retreat to the previously sighted camp. Defeated, we dinned that evening on flapjacks left over from brunch, topped with generous amounts of Irish Cream liqueur as a substitute for syrup.

The storm had drifted off by morning, leaving us with clear skies but muddy portages, the first one located in the northeast corner of Walter. The trail climbs steeply for approximately 40 rods (220 yd/200 m) before reaching Elizabeth Lake.

Paddling straight across to the small northern inlet on Elizabeth we then came to the next portage leading to the familiar Jesse Lake, a 147-rod (808 yd/740 m) mud bath with a few inclines along the way. Overall, however, it took less then 40 minutes to complete a double carry, with the only thing slowing us down being another moose standing in our way.

From Jesse we backtracked the rest of the morning to Batchewaung Bay, and then made the decision to end the day here rather then try to push hard all the way back to Nym Lake. Not only did this give us a good start for the long drive home the next day, it also gave us time to stop off at the main office to add two more black pins to the park map taped to the wall.

Jean Lake — Sturgeon Lake Loop

LENGTH: 5–6 days

PORTAGES: 22

LONGEST PORTAGE:
165 rods (908 yd/830 m)

DIFFICULTY: Advanced novice to intermediate canoe-tripping skills are required.

ACCESS: Nym Lake, located on the north side of the park. Drive east of Atikokan on Highway 11 and then turn south onto Nym Lake Road. From there it's another left onto a dirt road before the Y-intersection. The road ends at a designated parking lot and a short trail, beginning at the southeast corner of the parking lot, leading down to the Nym Lake dock. Take note that Nym Lake access point no longer has a gate-house onsite and that you now have to pick your permit up at the main office in Atikokan. To reach the main office, or park headquarters, drive north on Highway 11B, off Highway 11; it's on the right just as you enter the town.

ALTERNATIVE ACCESS: Dawson Trail Ranger Station, located at the main campground in the northeast corner of the park, just south off Highway 11. It's a 130-mile (210 km) drive west of Thunder Bay and 24 miles (39 km) east of Atikokan. From there you must paddle a day or two east on French and Pickerel Lakes to reach the portage into Jesse Lake.

TOPOGRAPHICAL MAPS: 52-B/5, B/12

FISHER MAPS: F-24, F-29, F-30

Andy's blueberry crumble sure beats porridge in the morning.

4 Sturgeon Lake / Olifaunt Lake Loop

IT SEEMED LIKE A GREAT IDEA AT THE TIME: rather than drive the two full days to reach the park, our group — a film crew working on a project for the Friends of Quetico — decided it would be less of a hassle to fly from Toronto to Thunder Bay. But after hauling all our gear through the airport, our flight was canceled; the next flight was forced to return to Toronto due to a mechanical failure (the front wheel was broken) after being airborne only ten minutes; then there was a three-hour delay before boarding the third flight. Even the rental car to shuttle us from the Thunder Bay airport to the desired access point in the park turned out to be a mix up, a convertible rather then the mini-van we had ordered. The rental company thought we wouldn't mind; that is, until we showed them the pile of camping and filming gear we had to transport. Andy, Kip and I had never wanted to begin a canoe trip so badly in our lives.

Thankfully our bad luck ended, and we were even able to have an outfitter from Atikokan (Canoe Canada) pick us up and drive us directly to the put-in on Pickerel Lake's Stanton Bay, which meant we had a full hour of daylight left to soak in our much-appreciated new surroundings (and locate a campsite before dark).

After such a long travel day, none of us were too keen on an early start the next day, but we couldn't afford to become windbound, something easily done on Pickerel Lake, so by 7:00 A.M. we left our comfortable campsite on the south end of Lookout Island, Kip and Andy in one canoe and me paddling solo, and headed southwest to locate the first portage in Pine Portage Bay.

By mid-morning it was rain that slowed our progress rather than wind, and as luck would have it, all three of us had stored our rain gear at the bottom of our packs. We were completely soaked by the time we reached the far side of the lake, where we stopped for brunch on Wetasi Island. The name Wetasi (yes, "wet ass"-i) was given to the island when a group of park rangers found shelter there after being drenched in a storm.

We definitely didn't welcome the poor weather, but the gray skies made for perfect light conditions for our first film project — capturing footage of the old boiler and other rusted machine parts from a sunken

An old boiler dating back to 1870.

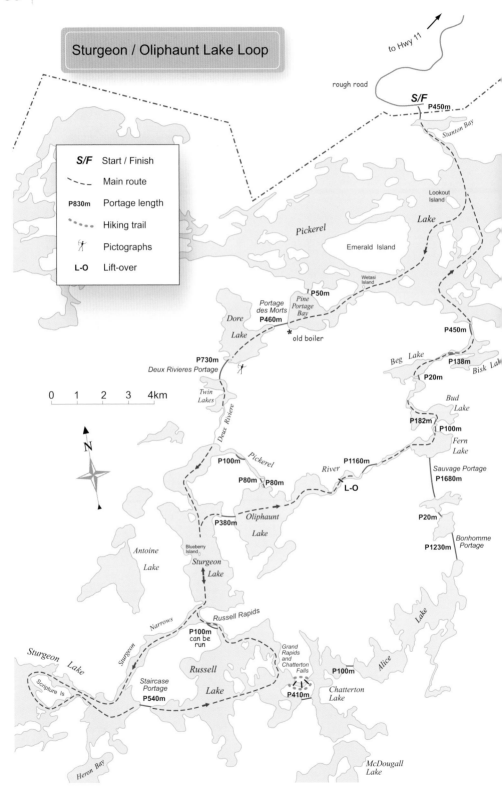

Sturgeon / Oliphaunt Lake Loop

to Hwy 11

rough road

S/F **P450m**

Stanton Bay

S/F	Start / Finish
- - -	Main route
P830m	Portage length
• • •	Hiking trail
🏹	Pictographs
L-O	Lift-over

Lookout Island

Pickerel

Emerald Island

Lake

Wetasi Island

P50m

Pine Portage Bay

Portage des Morts **P460m**

Dore Lake

* old boiler

P450m

Beg Lake

P730m

Deux Rivieres Portage

Twin Lakes

P138m

P20m

Bisk Lake

Bud Lake

P182m

P100m

Fern Lake

Deux Riviere

Pickerel

River

P1160m

Sauvage Portage

P1680m

0 1 2 3 4km

N

P100m

P80m **P80m**

L-O

P380m

Oliphaunt Lake

P20m

P1230m

Bonhomme Portage

Antoine Lake

Blueberry Island

Sturgeon Lake

Narrows

Russell Rapids

P100m can be run

Staircase Portage **P540m**

Russell Lake

Grand Rapids and Chatterton Falls

P100m

Alice Lake

Sturgeon Lake

Scripture Is

Sturgeon

P410m

Chatterton Lake

Heron Bay

McDougall Lake

tugboat left behind in the 1870s. The old junk is just off shore and to the left of the takeout for the 92-rod (406 yd/460 m) portage — labeled Portage de Morts after a voyageur was crushed to death by the weight of his own canoe and then buried nearby.

This portion of the trip is just teeming with history. This was the original route of the French-Canadian voyageurs, explored by Jacques de Noyon in 1688-89 and called the Kaministquia (or "Kam" for short) since it began by going up the Kaministquia River from Fort William (now Thunder Bay). It was soon replaced by the easier Grand Portage route, until a century later when the Grand Portage became American owned and the North West Trading Company "re-discovered" the Kaministquia out of necessity.

Historical records show that Portage de Morts was used extensively by the North West Company, rivals of the Hudson's Bay Company, to intercept Native traders heading north to do business on Hudson Bay. The Hudson Bay Company, who could no longer just wait for Native tribes to bring fur to them out on the Bay, moved inland and also made use of the Kaministquia route. Lord Selkirk, a chief stock-holder of the Hudson's Bay Company, who successfully disrupted the supply lines of the North West Company by sending new settlements out west, even ordered 100 voyageurs and 100 Swiss de Meuran mercenaries (and two cannons) over the Kaministquia in 1816. The armed force was to help win over a major conflict that, not surprisingly, began between the settlers and the North West Company. Nicholas Garry also traveled the Kaministquia route after being given the daunting diplomatic task of merging the North West and Hudson's Bay Companies after their amalgamation in 1821. The governor of the newly formed Hudson Bay Company, Sir George Simpson, and his bride, Lady Frances Ramsay Simpson, came this way in 1830, to reach Rainy Lake Post (renamed Fort Frances to honor his wife). And even the original detachment of the Royal Mounted Police took this portage while moving west.

The next portage, Deux Rivieres, is even more noteworthy in Canadian history. It's the original Dawson Trail — the first all-Canadian route built for the Red River settlers.

Simon Dawson, a surveyor for the Canadian government, traveled the old Kaministquia route while researching for the best all-Canadian way for settlers to head west. After his journey inland, Dawson came back believing the Kaministquia was the best choice, but the government was slow to agree. In fact, the only reason construction of the trail began was when the Red River settlements under the leadership of Louis Riel began to rebel and 1,400 soldiers had to be shipped out to keep peace (they were concerned over losing squatters rights under the transfer of the HBC territory to the Canadian government).

While our group carried across Deux Rivieres Portage, measuring 145 rods (798 yd/730 m) and located at the southwest end of Dore Lake, to the right of a

Taking a break from the heat of the day on Upper Sturgeon Lake.

small creek, the complexity of the real world, the one we so desperately tried to leave behind our first day out, gave us a visit. Halfway across with the initial load, an Ontario Provincial Police plane buzzed us. I didn't give it a second thought; that is until the turbo beaver buzzed us again, then again, and then again. It was obvious that the plane was trying to get our attention. We knew the plane had nowhere to land directly nearby, so Andy unpacked his satellite phone and I dialed up the park superintendent. He informed us they were indeed looking for someone, but not us. They were searching for an injured solo paddler in a red canoe (which I was mistaken for). The story goes that a group of American paddlers had an argument with one of their companions and, after punching him silly, left the guy back on Sturgeon Lake (supposedly thinking he was dead). They informed the police once they left the park, and search and rescue were now looking to see if he had survived the beating and was in the process of paddling out of the park.

The superintendent radioed the pilot to inform him I wasn't the victim, and the plane moved on. We later found out, however, that the man who was beaten by his pals did actually manage to paddle out alone, and that his fellow paddlers changed their story about the incident the moment they found out he was alive.

And to think, some campers believe bears are something to dread out in the wilds. It seems your canoe companions can be far more problematic.

Wanting to clear our heads of the whole tribulation, we quickly moved on, filming as we paddled through the weed-choked channel that separates upper and lower Twin Lakes and past another sequential gem in Quetico's history. Here, on June 9, 1843, John Henry Lefroy stopped to write down some "sentimental verses" on a sheet of birchbark. A pioneer in the study of terrestrial magnetism, Lefroy was on his way to search for the magnetic north pole at the time. Between 1842 and 1844 he traveled over 5,468 miles (8800 km) in the Canadian north while making magnetic and meteorological observations.

A shallow stream located at the southeast corner of the lake takes you out of Twin Lakes. It's been called Deux Riviere because it parallels the old extension of the Deux Riviere Portage, but its original name is more fitting: Grass River. The waterway is clogged with swamp grass, broken only by a couple of beaver dams that require a quick liftover. The stream widens the closer you get to the entrance to the top end of Sturgeon Lake but remains blocked by patches of sedge, reeds and wild rice almost all the way to the first island on the lake.

To the east the Pickerel River empties out into Sturgeon, and it was our original plan to loop back to Pickerel Lake, but the best part about canoe-tripping in Quetico is that once you've entered the park, you don't have to stick to your predetermined route plan. Our group had paddled quicker than anticipated and made more mileage, so we decided to continue south for an extra day or two.

Our second night's camp was set up to the left of where the lake narrows, on a perfect rock outcrop overlooking the large island north of Blueberry Island. It was an incredible spot, one of the best campsites I've ever stayed at in the park. We picked blueberries right around the fire circle and made blueberry turnovers for dessert. Andy even caught a few walleye for dinner by just casting a lure to the left of where Kip and I went in for a swim. Of course, we later found out that the site was one of the worst for nuisance bear encounters. Fortunately we never had a visit — and thankfully the news that it was a problem site was told to us *after* we had slept there.

The next day we lingered around camp until brunch, filming some scenes for the film. Kip had wanted to capture footage of me drudging through a nasty portage. The problem, however, is that we had yet to encounter a nasty one. It's not that we wouldn't eventually have a bad carry, or some other type of disaster along the way, but I think Kip was getting a little worried about how well the trip was going so far. So we faked getting lost on a "make-believe" trail directly behind the tent site. I know that sounds odd (and a bit unethical), but the filming Kip and I do together has always played on the misadventures of canoe-tripping. There's a reason for this, of course.

Some paddlers endorse the idea that canoe-tripping in a wilderness area is an absorbing, emotional, life-altering experience; it's a time of beauty, elegance and simplicity; it's even believed by some to bring about moments of spiritual awakening. And I agree. But our films, and my writing, always highlight the unpleasant experiences more than the pleasant ones. In fact, you'd even question why anyone would want to go paddling after watching, or reading, what happens to me out there — spending the day pushing a flimsy canoe across choppy water, carrying heavy gear across muddy portages, sleeping on the hard ground inside a tent the size of a dog house, and suffering the bites of black flies, mosquitoes, horseflies and those pesky no-see-ums.

There's the scenic splendor of wilderness canoeing, but if you ask any canoeist to reminisce about their favorite wilderness trip, it will always be their most difficult, grueling or nightmarish misadventure. Why is that?

After countless canoe-tripping experiences in remote areas, I've come to the conclusion that it's the real but often exaggerated dangers that help highlight your kinship with the wilderness. The more near disasters you experience and survive, the more connected to the land you feel, and perhaps the better you understand its importance to us.

We finished our filming just before noon and headed across Sturgeon but stopped just short of Sturgeon Narrows, drained by the extreme heat and a brisk wind that made forward progress nearly impossible. We had an extended rest, lying beneath a stand of stout pine and jumping in for a swim every 20 minutes. And then at 10:00 P.M. we headed out again, paddling over half the length of Sturgeon Lake during the calm, cool night air.

It was like a dreamscape. A three-quarter moon lighted the way, and we hugged the shoreline, listening to the water lapping against the rocks and letting it guide us. Kip filmed this experience, of course, but I didn't want him to. I wanted to stay in the moment, to soak in and mentally preserve these precious few hours of my life. It may sound selfish, but I didn't want it recorded on tape for others to view.

We backtracked on day four after having a half-day snooze on the third-largest island west of Sturgeon Lake's Scripture Island. Our camp that night was in Heron Bay, just southwest of Sturgeon Narrows. The campsite was Andy's idea. He was desperate to revisit a cluster of egg-shaped rocks that pop up out of the water to the south of the bay. Of course, Kip and I teased him all day about having to paddle out of our way just so he could view a bunch of white rocks that he once saw sticking out of the water. But when we witnessed the geological phenomena for ourselves, the mocking stopped immediately. This is one really cool-looking place in Quetico, rock deposits left over from the time when glaciers scoured the continental landmass and left massive erratic formations like the one in Heron Bay along its path.

Andy and I caught another load of walleye for dinner off the north shore and then watched as a bald eagle snatched the guts from where we filleted the fish, only to have a ring-billed gull snatch the leftover fish directly from the eagle's talons.

The side trip to see Andy's egg-shaped rock on Heron Bay was definitely worth it.

The wind was no longer an issue on day four, but the intense heat continued. At one point the thermometer clipped onto my pack in the front of the canoe read 104 degrees Fahrenheit. So once again we altered our route plans. We wanted to film Chatterton Falls where it plunges into Russell Lake and thought of heading south through Fred Lake, Cutty Creek, Nan Lake, Camel Lake, McDougall Lake and Chatterton Lake to reach Russell, but Andy had gone this way before and warned that pulling the canoes through the low water of Cutty Creek, and especially portaging through the marshy bits at the end of the 115-rod (632 yd/580 m) portage leading in to McDougall Lake, wouldn't be all that pleasant in such heat (even if Kip would finally get his "blooper" segments for the film). So we decided to backtrack again on Sturgeon and simply take a 107-rod (588 yd/540 m) portage directly in to Russell. Who knew that the latter portage would end up being one of the toughest and steepest trails in the park? (Turns out its nickname is "Staircase Portage.") Even after successfully clambering up and over the ridge separating Sturgeon and Russell without dying of heat stroke, we were forced to make an emergency camp seconds before an intense storm hit. Not just one of those five-minute blasts of lightning and heavy winds that happen in Quetico all the time, I'm talking a torrential downpour together with cyclone winds strong enough to rip one of our tents and our rain tarp to near shreds. Kip got enough "misadventure" footage to make a two-hour documentary.

We were slow to start up again the next morning, humbled I guess by the previous day's events. We were lucky, though. Our gear had weathered the storm worse than us, but the first-aid kit was only opened for Kip — and his injury had nothing to do with the squall. His toe was bitten by a snapping turtle while he soaked his feet at the shoreline.

The high temperatures were now gone. In fact it became quite cold (my thermometer now read 64 degrees Fahrenheit). The wind had also changed, but to our advantage. We were able to lash the two canoes together, sail all the way across Russell Lake and reach the base of Chatterton Falls by noon.

We set up camp at the bottom of the falls and spent the remainder of the day filming along a rough trail that makes its way along the south shore. The entire cascade is gorgeous, and the walk along this path is well worth the effort. I definitely wouldn't use this trail as a portage, however, or even the old portage found on the other side of the falls. The proper portage to Chatterton is found about a half mile (1 km) south of the falls, beginning on a sandy beach. There's a steep grade near the start and quite a few boulders blocking the 82-rod (450 yd/ 410 m) path, but it's far easier, and safer, than using the hiking trail around Chatterton Falls.

At the base of Chatterton you'll see the leftover debris from when 8,000 red and white pine logs were flushed downriver all at once, causing a massive jam. The incident happened in 1936, around the same time lumber baron J.A. Mathieu made a formal complaint about the lack of cutting available in the park. His grievances were quickly ignored after his company did nothing to remove the logjam at the falls. It was one of the biggest wastes of timber in northern Ontario's history. It also led to further protection of Quetico's forests. In 1941 Frank MacDougall became superintendent of Quetico and made major changes to protect timber in the park.

Our sixth day was the best yet. We headed out from our camp below Chatterton Falls just as the sun began burning off the morning mist. There wasn't even a slight breeze to hold us back while crossing Russell and Sturgeon Lakes, and we were able to flush easily down Russell Rapids, swift water that separates the two lakes, rather than use the 20-rod (110 yd/100 m) portage along the west bank (take note that the portage is plagued by poison ivy).

Before noon we found ourselves slogging across a flat but very muddy 75-rod (412 yd/380 m) portage to Olifaunt Lake. We raced across the bowl-shaped Olifaunt Lake, then paddled up the Pickerel River to have a late lunch at a short liftover to the left of a small drop.

From there the day got a little more difficult. The remaining portage of the day, a 230-rod (1,265 yd/1160 m) trail along the left bank of the Pickerel River, is a long, rugged carry. A few side trails lead off to sections of the river between rapids but only tease you into thinking you're getting close to the end. None of them are worth the hassle of loading and unloading gear. Just keep going. The view three-quarters the way along is wonderful, though, and makes the entire ordeal worthwhile.

At the put-in, our group met two Toronto paddlers, Collin McAdam and Joy Simmons (and their dog, Toby). Joy had canoed here for five weeks when she was a teenager and had always wanted to return. That was over 30 years ago. Collin, her husband of 27 years, had never been on a wilderness canoe trip in his life. Joy decided it was time to take him on one. Their story was so inspiring we thought it would be great idea to interview them for our film. They agreed, and as Kip prepared everything for the on-camera dialogue, we paid Joy and Collin's kindness back by portaging their first load.

Collin began by sharing his romantic view of Quetico: "Being in the wilderness is like a clean page — no distortion, no crap. There's just this beautiful randomness; every corner is different, every glance is different, the sun makes the same place different, depending on where it's at. But there's a constant, which is myself, my wife, and even Toby. There's a richness that just rains down on you. Back home, it is rare to spend 24 hours together. Our time out here is so precious."

Joy talked about the peacefulness, the extraordinary silence of it all, the meditative value of paddling across a lake, but she also connected these values to something very important in her life: "Looking at rocks that have been here for billions of years, it gives you a sense of your place in the longer scheme of things. I guess, for me, having been a survivor of breast cancer and just gone through a recent scare, there's something about that, just feeling that this earth will keep going, and I've had a wonderful life, and that my place in it is temporary, I'm passing through. It makes me feel very alive to be out here."

As we entered Fern Lake, we met a group volunteers who were on their way back from doing maintenance on the portage that leads to a chain of lakes to the south. Seconds into the conversation Kip asked them for an interview, too. It was getting late, so we decided to do it in the morning, back on the portage. The volunteers chose the centre island to camp on, and we picked a rock point to the southwest. I think they got the better site. Ours had seen little use, and with a wasp nest directly beside the fire ring, we were forced to cook our dinner on a camp stove and pitch our tents well back in the bush.

I guess our tents were a little too far back in the bush. The morning sun, which usually wakes us up bright and early, didn't hit the sides of our tents until after eight, and all three of us were still snug in our bags when a couple of the volunteers paddled over to offer us freshly brewed coffee and toasted cinnamon bannock.

By 9:30 A.M. Kip had the camera set up at the section of trail where the volunteers were cutting and placing logs across a giant swamp. It was an excellent backdrop for deliberating the reasons for being here, working for free. Russ James, a councilor who had been with Camp Kooch-i-ching since he was ten,

It sure beats having to portage. Andy Baxter on the Pickerel River.

started it off: "It was just time to pay back all the others who worked on the portages before me. Back at camp we have a saying above our mantel: 'Chop your own wood and it will warm you twice.'"

All their statements reflected the idea of how precious and unique Quetico is, but the statement made by councilor Matt Brown from Kentucky just blew me away: "Preserving a place like this really allows us all that experience, that contact with nature that's slipping away from our modern society. These kids could be at home playing Nintendo or doing whatever, and they all say after the trip, 'You know, that's what I wanted to be doing — and my friends, they're getting cheated by not having it.' I hope my own kids enjoy Quetico, and I hope they remember what Henry David Thoreau said: 'I went to the woods because I wished to live deliberately, to front only the essential facts of life, and to see if I could not learn what it had to teach, and not, when I came to die, discover that I had not lived.'"

We helped the volunteers with the trail for a couple more hours before heading off. It felt good to lend a hand, but we also had to reach Pickerel Lake by the end of the day since our plane was scheduled to leave Thunder Bay at 2:00 P.M. the following day.

It was a quick paddle across to the north shore, where the Pickerel River emptied into Fern Lake, and we simply waded up the rapids rather than take the grown-over 20-rod (110 yd/100 m) portage found to the right. Then, as the river twists right towards a stunted cascade, we pulled up to the 36-rod (198 yd/182 m) portage on the left. It was a gorgeous carry alongside tumbling waterfalls decorated with giant pine and old gnarly white cedar trees.

From there we paddled west and then north on Bud Lake, which is simply a widening of the Pickerel River. The banks narrowed at times, bringing us close to the remnants of an old burn and forcing us to push against a strong current at times. Only once did we actually have to get out of the canoes and carry, that was over a slab of rock, for 4 rods (22 yd/20 m), just to the far right of where a small chute links Bud Lake with Beg Lake.

The route went east now, heading into Bisk Lake by way of a 27-rod (148 yd/138 m) portage to the right of another scenic falls. It's an easy carry, with only a slight rise along the first quarter of the trail.

The last portage of the day was only a short paddle up the northern inlet of Bisk Lake. Here a 90-rod (495 yd/450 m) trail runs along the left side of where the Pickerel River flushes out of Pickerel Lake. We were able to shorten the carry a bit by paddling a few extra strokes upstream.

The portage ends at a giant concrete dam built in 1872 by Simon Dawson and the Dominion Government to raise the water levels between the French and Pickerel Lakes to allow passage of steamboats carrying soldiers and settlers out to the Red River Settlements. The dam was rebuilt in 1927 by timber barons Shevlin-Clarke to raise the water again and run logs down the Quetico River. It was washed out during spring flood in 1941, and the concrete structure wasn't built

It's a camp rule that if the person who carries the lightest pack complains the most, they will get a few rocks tossed in when they're not looking.

Volunteers from Camp Kooch-i-ching spend two weeks cleaning up canoe routes in Quetico, and as a reward they receive a two-week canoe trip in the park: Their motto: "Chop your own wood and it will warm you twice."

until 1956. Then, after years of debate over the use of dams in the park, it was decided in the late 1970s to gradually remove the stop logs to allow the French and Pickerel Lakes to return to their natural levels.

It was late in the afternoon and we considered camping next to the dam. There were places to put the tents, but the site itself wasn't attractive. Besides, it was the last night of our trip and we wanted to end it somewhere more charming than alongside a big slab of cement. So we continued on, pushing hard against a steady wind out of the northwest. And it wasn't long before we started to regret our decision — especially me. I was already exhausted from paddling solo all day and now I had to battle a heavy chop.

To escape the more open part of Pickerel Lake we headed directly across from the dam, then took a weedy channel to the northeast. Our map showed the small inlet as unnavigable — which is probably true most of the time — but we managed to push our way through to the next bay.

This was the first time on the trip that we had trouble finding an unoccupied site. It was also the worst time for this to happen to us. I would have even settled for any flat piece of land to curl up on for the night, but there was nowhere to stop.

We continued on for another hour or so before we were forced to settle for a miniature island near where we had stopped our first night out. There was a small site, but a recent windstorm had blown several trees down, leaving limited space. We managed. Kip placed his tent between two fallen jack pine, and we squeezed ours uncomfortably close to the lakeshore.

Being surrounded by downed timber, we decided against having a campfire that night. Instead we lit a couple of candles, poured a double shot of rum into our camp mugs, then used up the remainder of the camera battery to view all the footage Kip had filmed throughout the trip. Here we were watching our work directly on site, equipped with a high-definition digital camera complete with a computerized editing suite. We couldn't imagine what poor Ken Buck, Bill Mason's cameraman, had to go through during their filming excursions back in the 1970s and '80s. Ken and Bill worked on a number of canoe films (*Path of the Paddle, Song of the Paddle, Waterwalker*) using only a 16 mm camera. The technology of the time meant that the footage couldn't be viewed until weeks after the trip.

The method of capturing what's out here had clearly changed over time, but the art of documenting wilderness canoe trips had not. What we caught on camera during our trip was remarkably similar to what Ken and Bill shot decades earlier. It was Bill Mason himself who said after filming *Waterwalker*: "Film can be deceiving, but when it comes to the beauty of the world out here, the camera has not lied."

Sturgeon Lake / Olifaunt Lake Loop

LENGTH: 5–6 days

PORTAGES: 10

LONGEST PORTAGE: 230 rods (1,265 yd/1160 m)

DIFFICULTY: Advanced novice to intermediate canoe-tripping skills are required.

ACCESS: Stanton Bay, located about three-quarters of the way down Pickerel Lake, is used to avoid the long paddle across French and Pickerel Lakes. Permits must first be picked up at Dawson Trail Ranger Station, then drive west on Highway 11 for 6.5 miles (10 km), a half-mile (1 km) past the intersection of Highway 11 and 633. It's a very rough gravel road, so it takes approximately 40 minutes to reach the small parking area. From here you have to portage 90 rods (495 yd/450 m) to the lake. The portage is located just to the right of the upper right-hand corner of the parking lot. At time of publication, only Canadian paddlers can legally park here overnight. If you are a non-resident, you must use a Canadian outfitter to drop you off there. (I'm just as confused about this policy as you are).

ALTERNATIVE ACCESS: Dawson Trail Ranger Station, located at the main campground in the northeast corner of the park, just south off Highway 11. It's a 130-mile (210 km) drive west of Thunder Bay and 24 miles (39 km) east of Atikokan.

TOPOGRAPHICAL MAPS: 52-B/5, 52-B/6, 52-B/11, 52-B/12

FISHER MAPS: F-24, F-25, F-30

5 International Canoe Derby Route

A COUPLE OF YEARS AGO my publishing company sent me on an extended speaking tour. In two months, I had to give close to 20 radio and television interviews and over 30 presentations. I loved the attention, but the calendar said it was June, and it seemed everyone except me was out paddling. Working too hard and never finding time to canoe is one thing, but the idea of working so hard as a canoeist that you find no time to canoe, that's just stupid!

I stopped for a coffee at a roadside café just prior to one of my speaking engagements, and in the parking lot was a group of canoeists meeting up for a trip. As I walked by them, I could hear the excitement in their voices, feel their enthusiasm, even smell the wood smoke on their gear as they loaded it into their shuttle vehicles. The whole scene made me jealous, and after my presentation that night I phoned the promotions department and asked them to put everything on hold. The next day I packed up and went tripping in Quetico.

The route I planned was one I've always wanted to try: the one that retraces the historic International Canoe Derby. The record time for this 200-mile (322 km) round-trip is less than 24 hours. Of course, I had no interest in beating the record. This was a trip I wanted to savor, taking ten days to paddle from French Lake, near Atikokan, to Fall Lake, in Ely, and back again. The original race, in 1962, was done in reverse, but it was the 1963 version I was most interested in. I had recently read William N. Rom's book *Canoe Country Wilderness* and was quite taken by his story of competing in the race that year with high-school chum Ropie Mackie.

Rom and Mackie didn't win the derby in 1963. They came in ninth place (43 hours). But the story of the trip was inspiring. Their physical endurance was remarkable: just to get their canoe to the starting line, prior to the race, they first paddled from Ely to Atikokan. Rom's remarks on how their wild surroundings motivated them the entire way added real flavor to the trip, and that's the part I was hooked on. I wasn't interested in replicating the race or beating any records; my interest was in the larger intention behind the race — to paddle across Quetico.

Not only was the timeline of my trip completely different than Rom and Mackie's, I also packed dissimilar equipment. I had a lightweight Kevlar canoe and fancy meals. They had a "94-pound Chestnut-model canvas canoe and precooked steak and assorted candies." In fact, the only similarities between our respective trips were the high winds and rough water waiting for me at the starting gate, the main beach at the Dawson Trail Campground.

It took me two full days rather then the usual half-day to paddle from the east end of French Lake to near Lookout Island on Pickerel Lake, at which point I opted for changing the route slightly. Rom and Mackie had gone to the far west end of Pickerel and then south to Chatterton Lake by way of Pine Portage, Dore Lake, Sturgeon Lake, and then Russell Lake. I cut corners by heading down the Pickerel River and making use of the two portages cut by two other racers, Meany and Tetrault, back in 1964.

According to the rules of the race, the paddlers could take any route they wanted through the park as long as it was laid out between the start and finish lines. The course Rom and Mackie took was used by the majority of participants because it was believed to be the quickest way. However, Joe Meany and Eugene Tetrault spent 12 days prior to the race cutting two trails through a giant mud-filled bog between Fern and Alice Lakes. The portages gave them their victory in 1964 with a time of 38 hours, 50 minutes, and 25 seconds.

The wind finally calmed down on my third day out, and it took only a few hours of easy paddling to reach Fern Lake. The 90-rod (495 yd/450 m) portage to the right of Pickerel River Dam was a quick carry. So was the 27-rod (148 yd/138 m) carry to the left of the falls, between Bisk and Beg Lakes. Then I kept with the gentle current of the Pickerel River and paddled through the narrow channel leading to Bud Lake, getting out of the canoe only once to lift over to the far left of a small chute. From Bud to Fern Lakes, there was a rockbound but rel-

My intention on retracing the International Canoe Derby route wasn't to beat any records; it was to create an excuse to paddle across Quetico.

Keeping your feet dry while crossing the Sauvage Portage is next to impossible.

atively straightforward 36-rod (198 yd/182 m) portage to the right of a tumbling cascade, followed by a gravel swift that can easily be navigated (if you don't want to get your feet wet, there's a short but rough portage located to the left, and it ends at a campsite).

It was just before 1:00 P.M. when I started my trip across the first of the two portages cut in 1964. The 336-rod (1,848 yd/1690 m) trail is named Sauvage Portage, shortened from Maux Jit Sauvage, and named after Joe Meany.

Locating the start of the Sauvage Portage has always been an issue, even more so if you're heading the opposite way. Racers competing in the 2003 Raid of the North Extreme took this route, and more than one group found themselves bush-whacking from Fern Lake instead of taking the trail.

Luckily, I had been here before, the same summer that a group of Quetico volunteers were working on the portage, so not only was it easy to find the takeout, but also the trail was somewhat cleared out by then. The first part of the trail is not really an issue as long as the blow-downs are cleared away; it's the giant swamp about three-quarters the way along that's the problem. You can literally find yourself waist deep in boot-sucking mud. At one point I found it easier to load my packs into the canoe and push everything across the wet area, jumping from one mound of swamp grass to the next. Thankfully, the volunteer maintenance crew had laid a row of logs down horizontally over the worst of the mucky parts.

It was after 4:00 P.M. by the time I made it across the Sauvage Portage. I knew the second trail — measuring 245 rods (1,348 yd/1230 m) and titled Bonhomme Portage ("good man") for Eugene Tetrault — wasn't as bad as Sauvage; it only had a steep section at the takeout, a giant beaver dam you had to carefully balance yourself across, then another slightly steep downhill section near the put-in. But I decided to end the day early and take advantage of having this remote spot all to myself. I paddled the first of two unnamed lakes prior to Alice Lake and carried across a short 6-rod (33 yd/30 m) portage beginning in a miniature lagoon and extending to the right of a small creek. I then pitched my tent on the south side of a central island in the second unnamed lake, and celebrated my solitude by pouring an extra shot of Irish Cream in my evening tea.

The next morning was gorgeous. The first hour-and-a-half was spent slogging across the lengthy Bonhomme Portage, where I barely escaped hundreds of wasps that had nested in the roots of an old tree toppled near the takeout. After that I was able to relax and spend the rest of the morning slowly making my way across Alice Lake. I even stopped for brunch on a quick 20-rod (110 yd/100 m) portage linking the southwestern bay of Alice Lake to Chatterton Lake. From there I kept close to the left shoreline, finding my way to where the Maligne River tumbles over Split Rock Falls.

The portage, which begins at a slab of granite, wasn't a bad carry by comparison to Sauvage or Bonhomme, but the 84-rod (462 yd/420 m) trail did have a slight incline right after the takeout and a maze of giant boulders to balance gingerly across near the put-in on Keats Lake.

Keats Lake is named after poet John Keats, who died of tuberculosis in 1821 at the young age of 25. Though his life was short, the romantic poet was extremely prolific, writing countless classics (Quetico lakes Isabella and Agnes may have been titled after his poems "Isabella" and "The Eve of St. Agnes"). Ironically, Keats had this engraved on his tombstone: "Here lies one whose name is writ in water." I guess he got his wish.

Nearby lakes Chatterton and Shelley were also named after famous poets, both of whom were strong followers of Keats' work. Chatterton also died at an early age, with Keats dedicating his poem "Endymion" to him. At 17 he swallowed arsenic mixed with water to either commit suicide or to cure himself of venereal disease. He spent an impoverished life, half starved most of the time, and his best work was based on the fabricated writings of a fictitious fifteenth-century Bristol monk named Thomas Rowley. P.B. Shelley wrote a long elegy for Keats entitled *Adonais*. Shelley drowned during a sailing trip, and when his body washed ashore, a book of Keats' poetry was found in his pocket. What emphasized his love of Keats' work further, however, was the discovery of his heart, taken from his cremated body by his wife and wrapped in Shelley's famous eulogy to Keats.

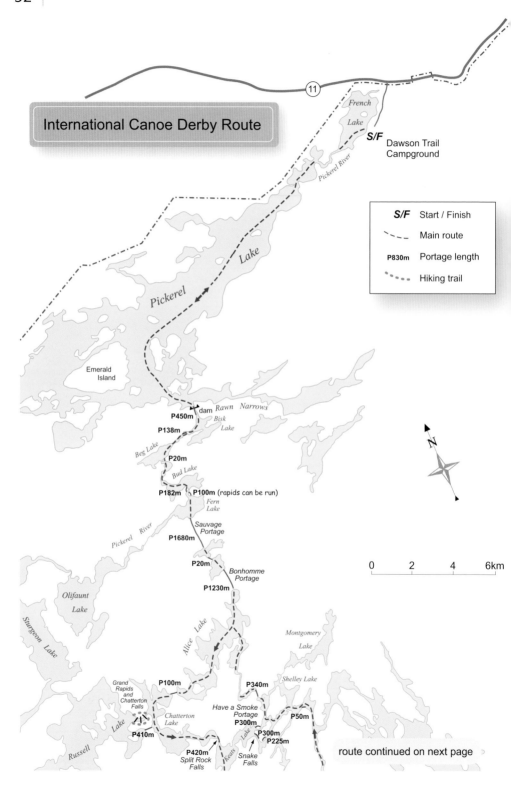

International Canoe Derby Route

S/F Dawson Trail Campground

Legend

S/F	Start / Finish
- - -	Main route
P830m	Portage length
••••	Hiking trail

French Lake

Pickerel River

Pickerel Lake

Emerald Island

P450m dam Rawn Narrows
Bisk Lake
P138m
Beg Lake
P20m
Bud Lake
P182m P100m (rapids can be run)
Fern Lake
Sauvage Portage
P1680m
Pickerel River
P20m
Bonhomme Portage
P1230m

Olifaunt Lake

Sturgeon Lake

Alice Lake

Montgomery Lake

Shelley Lake

Grand Rapids and Chatterton Falls
P100m
P340m
Have a Smoke Portage
P300m
P50m
Russell Lake
P410m
Chatterton Lake
P300m
P225m
P420m
Split Rock Falls
Keats Lake
Snake Falls

N

| 0 | 2 | 4 | 6km |

route continued on next page

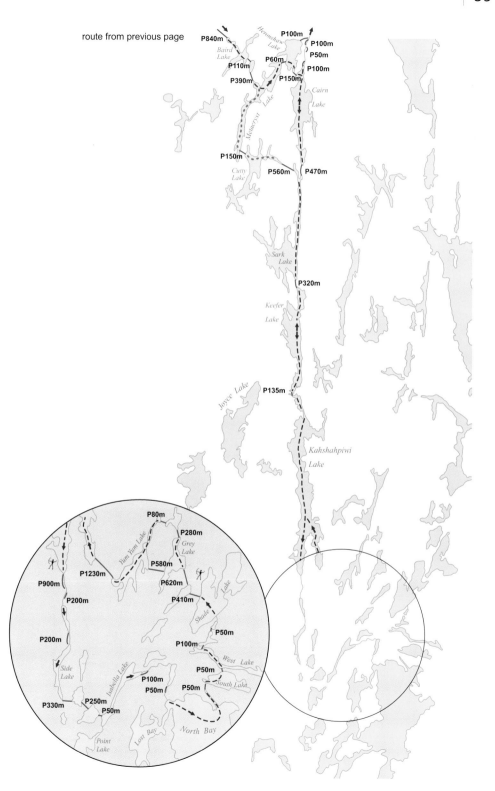

route from previous page

Heronshaw Lake

P840m

P100m
P100m
P50m
P100m

Baird Lake

P110m
P60m
P390m
P150m

Cairn Lake

P150m

Metuewisi Lake

P150m
P560m
P470m

Cutty Lake

Sark Lake

P320m

Keefer Lake

Joyce Lake

P135m

Kahshahpiwi Lake

P80m
P280m

Yum Yum Lake

Grey Lake

P900m
P1230m
P580m
P200m
P620m
P410m

Shade Lake

P200m

P50m

Side Lake

P100m

West Lake

Isabella Lake

P100m
P50m

South Lake

P330m
P250m
P50m
P50m
P50m

Lost Bay

North Bay

Point Lake

Having a smoke at the end of Have-a-Smoke Portage isn't recommended for nonsmokers.

The normal route from Keats Lake heads east for a while around Snake Falls, where it's best to use the relatively easy 75-rod (412 yd/380 m) "Have-a-Smoke" Portage on the north side rather than the two shorter but steeper trails to the south. From here it's across Shelley Lake and then up Kahshahpiwi Creek to Cairn Lake. But rather than taking the straightforward route, I decided to link up with Cairn by paddling and portaging south of Keats, through Baird and Heronshaw Lakes. It meant extra portaging, but I didn't have to worry about paddling against the current up the Kahshahpiwi Creek and, more important, I'd once again get into rarely used parts of the park.

A 167-rod (918 yd/840 m) portage at the very southeast end of Keats, to the left of a small creek complete with a miniature waterfall, took me to the top end of Baird Lake. It was hardy used and rather steep, with extremely muddy parts during the last quarter. The lake itself was fairly cloudy, and the campsite I chose wasn't exactly a true campsite, just a flat spot in the bush to place my tent, but I was alone again and that's all I wanted.

I awoke to a misty rain and ended up brewing my morning coffee under the protection of the rain tarp before packing the packs. I made sure to pull on my rain pants as well as my jacket. The full rain apparel wasn't entirely for the rain. I was more concerned about keeping dry while slogging through the wet underbrush along the two portages out of Baird: a 22-rod (121 yd/110 m) trail to an unnamed pond, followed by a 78-rod (430 yd/390 m) trail leading to Metacryst Lake.

Despite the full rain gear, I was totally soaked through by the time I completed the two carries, and the morning drizzle stopped the moment I reached the put-in at Metacryst. In hindsight I should have pushed on the day before and camped here rather than Baird Lake. Not only would I have kept dry, but Metacryst is also a more scenic lake. Not far from the end of the portage were two nice campsites and directly across from them, a large stand of old-growth white pine intermixed with patch of mature jack pine.

Metacryst has one of the few stands of old-growth pine in Quetico. Only three percent of the park's forest is made up of this ancient white pine, with four and a half percent red pine. This particular stand is even noted in the Wildland's League's *Ancient Forest Exploration Guide*, where it is compared to more noteworthy sites in Ontario's Temagami and Algoma regions.

After a quick brunch of cinnamon bannock and tea on the second of the two sites, a 12-rod (66 yd/60 m) portage, located in Metacryst Lake's very northeastern tip, took me to Heronshaw Lake. From there I paddled to the end of the most southern bay on Heronshaw to locate a 30-rod (165 yd/150 m) portage leading to the top end of Cairn Lake, close to the beginning of Kahshahpiwi Creek.

It would have been possible for me to head southeast on Metacryst Lake, linking up with Cutty and Sark Lakes by two portages: a rarely used 30-rod (165 yd/150 m) trail alongside a creek and a 110-rod (605 yd/560 m) trail with a number of up-and-down ridges and a few mud holes in between. However, Cairn Lake is a body of water that shouldn't be missed. It has a stunning backdrop of dramatic cliffs, creeks with miniature cascades tumbling into tranquil bays, and some of the nicest island campsites Quetico has to offer. In fact, this entire chain of lakes (Cairn, Sark, Keefer, Kahshahpiwi) is situated along an old geological fault line, and each lake is almost a mirror image of the other.

Less than an hour after the morning drizzle stopped, a strong breeze came out of the north and gave me a much-appreciated tailwind on my way south. I made great time and even sailed large sections of Sark and Keefer Lakes. The only thing that slowed my progress was getting out and portaging between each of the four lakes: 94 rods (517 yd/470 m) connect Cairn to Sark; 64 rods (352 yd/320 m) connect Sark to Keefer; and 27 rods (148 yd/135 m) connect Keefer to Kahshahpiwi. All run alongside picturesque rapids and none of the carries are significant; they are just nice places to get out of the cramped canoe and stretch your legs.

It was close to 8:00 P.M. by the time I made camp on the north end of Kahshahpiwi Lake. I wasn't tired. In fact, I would have paddled further if it weren't for all the prime campsites available to me shortly after the last portage. I had seen only a few other paddlers between Cairn and Kahshahpiwi Lakes, and now it felt as if I had the park all to myself. It had been an incredible day, really;

one of those times in canoe country when you feel completely connected to the landscape. I knew I had done the right thing in swapping my lecture tour for a tent and a canoe.

The next morning I counted 18 canoes paddling toward my campsite, enough that I lost any desire to continue all the way to Ely. I had planned to paddle the U.S. portion of the route and had even obtained a Remote Border Crossing Permit, but seeing the crowds head across the lake that morning I came to the conclusion that spending a couple of days traveling one of the busiest sections of Quetico-Superior country, just to duplicate a notable canoe race, wasn't worth it. Change of plan: my goal was now to reach Basswood Lake's north bay before turning back to the Dawson Trail Campground on French Lake. At least by going this far I could claim a successful crossing of Quetico Park.

It took me a good part of the morning to paddle to the south end of Kahshahpiwi Lake. I stopped for an early lunch after taking on the 180-rod (990 yd/900 m) portage at the bottom end of the lake. The trail went up a slight incline at first and then ended in a swampy pond. I was slightly confused as to the proper route to take from there. My map showed a short trail to the left of the pond. I couldn't locate it, so I ended up bearing to the right, putting in beside a granite cliff face, paddling across the pond, and then lifting over a beaver dam to reach an unnamed lake.

The unnamed lake was weed-choked and shallow, but the 40-rod (220 yd/200 m) portage on the other side, linking up with Side Lake, wasn't too bad. The next portage, however, was insanely steep. The 65-rod (358 yd/330 m) trail begins on the very south end of Side Lake but splits close to the takeout. I took the left fork and climbed up and over a large mound of granite to another unnamed lake. From there, I stuck to the right-hand shoreline, made my way up a shallow creek clogged with dead-heads, and then began the 50-rod (275 yd/250 m) portage to the left of an old beaver dam. And waiting for me on the other side was a 10-rod (55 yd/50 m) trail to the right of a creek entering the lower end of Isabella Lake.

Most paddlers reach Basswood's north bay by continuing south from Isabella, but I turned left after the 10-rod (55 yd/50 m) portage and paddled north up the pencil-shaped lake. From here, I turned south by heading to the far end of the most northeastern bay and taking a well-defined 20-rod (110 yd/100 m) portage up and over a rock outcrop to a shallow creek. The channel was shallow and blocked by several beaver dams. The creek bed, however, was sandy and allowed for easy wading through the unmanageable parts. Eventually the route twisted increasingly to the south and ended with a short section of swift water that I lined through rather than taking the 10-rod (55 yd/50 m) portage to the right.

I was lucky enough to find one of the island campsites free near the entrance to the northeastern bay and celebrated my victory in making it all the way across the park by cooking up an extra batch of cinnamon rolls in my Outback Oven

Baking dessert is one of my biggest pleasures while out on a canoe trip.

and smearing them with half a tube of white frosting, with little bits of shredded chocolate sprinkles.

I also toasted Canadian surveyor and mapmaker David Thompson with a mug of rum and tea. Thompson was responsible for making this portion of canoe country part of Canada.

For a number of years the boundary between Canada and the United States, which is also now the boundary between Quetico and the Boundary Waters, was disputed by both sides. Both countries agreed that the line would be drawn along the main travel route. The problem was, no one could decide on the main travel route. The Americans claimed it was the Kaministikwia, along the Pickerel and Sturgeon Lakes, and down the Maligne River to Lac la Croix. The Canadians claimed it was the Grand Portage route, along the Pigeon River to Lac la Croix. It's true that the Kaministikwia route was the first to be used by the French fur-traders, but the Grand Portage quickly became more popular because it was the easier route.

David Thompson's maps of 1823-24 settled the argument. He remarked that the voyageurs had to be "coaxed and bribed" to use the more difficult Kaministikwia route and that the Grand Portage to Lac la Croix was the "customary waterway" because it had more navigable water. The interesting part, however, was that the Grand Portage route only had more water when Thompson went through because of unusually high water levels. If he had traveled through later on in the season Quetico country may well have been part of the United States.

Leaving your stinky boots outside the tent at night is always a good idea.

My route back north to Kahshahpiwi Lake was different then the way I came. I left my island campsite and headed north along a shallow creek, portaging a short 10 rods (55 yd/50 m) to reach South Lake. Another quick carry of the same length, to the northeast and beside where a small cascade tumbles into South Lake, took me into West Lake. And keeping to the right hand shore of West Lake I found two more portages leading into Shade Lake. The first was approximately 15-20 rods (80 to 100 m), going up a short incline and nearby another small waterfall, and a really easy 10-rod (55 yd/50 m) portage. It was marked on my map on the left-hand side of a creek, but I was able to do a quick liftover and paddle the rest of the way.

Shade Lake had some interesting Native pictographs along a cliff face to the far northeast corner of the lake. The paintings are set back from the shoreline and a quite faded, so it took me awhile to locate them. It's also said they depict two separate Thunderbirds, mystic creatures who are responsible for fierce storms. However, I found them so much more abstract from other Thunderbird paintings I've come across in the north that I'd have to guess that the artist had something else completely in mind when he placed them here hundreds of years ago.

Next I backtracked about a mile from the Shade Lake pictograph site to begin a 82-rod (451 yd/410 m) portage to a good-size unnamed lake, and then a 124-rod (682 yd/620 m) portage almost immediately to the right, leading into Grey Lake. The 82-rod (451 yd/410 m) carry wasn't a problem but the 124 rods (682 yd/620 m) into Grey began and ended with a steep slope and a beaver meadow filled with boot-sucking mud in between.

To the left of the last portage, my map showed a 115-rod (632 yd/580 m) portage leading into Yum Yum Lake (named after a character Gilbert and Sullivan's opera *The Mikado*). However, I wasn't overly keen on slogging through mud again, so I decided to take the long way around by paddling north through Armin Lake. I'm not sure how difficult the 115-rod (632 yd/580 m) trail would have been, but the two portages in and out of Armin, measuring 55 and 15 rods (302 and 82 yd/280 and 80 m) were pretty easy.

What came next definitely wasn't. The lengthy 245-rod (1,348 yd/1230 m) portage linking the far end of Yum Yum with Kahshahpiwi Lake was absolutely terrible. I'd read up on it prior to the trip. In Sigurd Olson's book *Songs of the North*, he lists this as one of the nastiest portages: "fairly level at first, then goes down into a swampy beaver flowage where in the spring the water may be waist deep, and then over a high mountainous ridge." His account is pretty accurate, except it begins almost immediately with a swampy takeout, followed shortly after by an abrupt muddy slope. On a plus note, Olson was also right when he added, "The view from the ridge of the knifelike gash that is Kashapiwi and its high shores, with the realization that only those who are willing to take a punishment of the grueling trail may see it, is reward enough."

Portaging along the upper Maligne River.

The portage didn't get any worse, but it didn't get any better, either. By the time I reached Kahshahpiwi, I made the decision to paddle to the familiar site on the north end of the lake and call it a day.

The return trip to Dawson Trail Campground on French Lake took me another four days, and my way back across the park was only slightly different than my way in. From Cairn Lake I continued down Kahshahpiwi Creek to Shelley Lake and then Keats Lake. The route change required only four short portages. All were on the left bank, except for the second, and all measured between 10 to 20 rods (55 to 80 yd/50 to 100 m). Some of the rapids the portages avoided could possibly be run or lined during good water conditions. I also opted to retrace my steps across the Bonhomme and Sauvage portages instead of taking the Chatterton-Russell-Sturgeon-Twin Lakes-Dore Lake-Pine Portage route back to Pickerel and French Lakes. But rather than enter Alice Lake from the west side, I paddled to the northwest corner of Shelley Lake to take a shallow creek into the south end of Alice. The 68-rod (374 yd/340 m) portage to the small pond before the creek was okay, but it soon became a bit of a slog going up the creek that flows from Alice Lake to the pond. It was navigable at first, where the creek comes in to the far right side of a marshy area on the west end of the pond (make sure not to take the separate creek coming in from the left). A quarter of the way up, however, I had to lift over boulders and then drag the canoe up a shallow, mucky stretch for a good 20 minutes until I reached a beaver dam at the entrance to Alice Lake.

The next-to-last night was spent on the familiar island site on the unnamed lake after the Bonhomme Portage, where I ceremoniously drank the last of my Irish Cream. I spent the last night halfway down Pickerel Lake.

When I returned, it was back to my long-winded speaking tour, but now I had new energy, and definitely new insights. I had even created a new rule for myself: For every talk I give on the values of wilderness canoe-tripping, I must go out and paddle the equivalent. So far, I've managed to stick to that rule, spending one day on the water for every lecture given. Who could complain about a job like that?!

International Canoe Derby Route

LENGTH: 7–8 days

PORTAGES: 46

LONGEST PORTAGE: 230 rods (1,265 yd/1160 m) DIFFICULTY: Intermediate canoe-tripping skills are required.

ACCESS:
Dawson Trail Ranger Station, located at the main campground in the northeast corner of the park, just south off Highway 11. It's a 130-mile (210 km) drive west of Thunder Bay and 24 miles (39 km) east of Atikokan.

ALTERNATIVE ACCESS: Stanton Bay, located about three-quarters the way down Pickerel Lake, is used to avoid the long paddle across French and Pickerel Lakes. Permits must first be picked up at Dawson Trail Ranger Station. Then, drive west on Highway 11 for 6.5 miles (10 km), a half mile (1 km) past the intersection of Highway 11 and 633. It's a rough gravel road and it that takes approximately 40 minutes to reach the small parking area. From here you have to portage 90 rods (450 m) to the lake.

The portage is located just to the right of the upper right-hand corner of the parking lot. At this point, only Canadian paddlers can legally park overnight here. If you are a non-resident, you must use a Canadian outfitter to drop you off there. (I'm just as confused about this policy as you are).

Also, if you're planning on entering through the United States, you can access through Prairie Portage Ranger Station. It's reached by paddling north on Moose, Newfound and Sucker Lakes, and then portaging 28 rods (154 yd/140 m) over to Basswood Lake. The cabin is to your right. But before that, you must drive northeast out of the American town of Ely, Minnesota. Take Highway 169 (Fernberg Road) and then Moose Lake Road. It's 19 miles (31 km) from Ely to the public launch.

TOPOGRAPHICAL MAPS: 52-B/3, 52-B/4, 52-B/5, 52-B/6, 52-B/11

FISHER MAPS:
F-10, F-11, F-18, F-25, F-30

6 Poohbah Lake Route

THE STORY BEHIND HOW QUETICO became a forest reserve in 1909 and a provincial park in 1913 is a complex one, full of politics and opposing interests. It was an impassioned debate, and there's definitely no shortage of literature on the subject. The most compelling writings, in my opinion, are the journal entries of Ernest Oberholtzer from his initial canoe trip in the park. "Ober" was a key figure in the preservation of the Quetico-Superior wilderness, and an advocate of the park's conception. He canoed Quetico not long after it was established, and noted in his diary the pleasures he found along the way. To me, his journal not only presents a definitive view of Quetico during its initial development, it demonstrates the real reason why this chunk of wilderness deserves protection in the first place.

Oberholtzer and his Native guide, Billy Magee (Taytahpahwaywiton, meaning "Far Distant Echo"), spent August and September on a route beginning in the northwestern end, near Lerome Lake, and finished up in the southeast, at Gunflint Lake. To retrace their exact route would be a great trip, not to mention an exceptional way to celebrate the upcoming 100th anniversary of the park in 2009. Realistically, however, with the average canoe trip nowadays lasting only a week, not a month or two, you might instead choose to visit Oberholtzer's favorite lake — Poohbah Lake. After all, *where* Oberholtzer and Magee went in 1909 isn't as important as *why* they went: to celebrate the birth of one of North America's largest protected wilderness areas, Quetico Provincial Park.

Oberholtzer's route to Poohbah was via Lerome, Cirus and Beaverhouse Lakes, then down the Quetico River, up the Namakan River to Lac la Croix, and finally up the Maligne River. To keep your trip to five days, begin at Lac la Croix's northern access point. Take note, however, that there's no direct way to the Lac la Croix ranger station. It can be reached by driving to the remote Native village of Lac la Croix, using a 50-mile (79 km), two-hour, seasonally maintained bush road south of Highway 11, just west of Atikokan. There is a public launch area on the far side of the town, but most paddlers book a shuttle boat from Crane Lake access or a bushplane flight from outfitters either outside of Atikokan or Ely (boats and planes are allowed to land on Lac la Croix, close to the mouth of the Maligne River). Some canoeists even paddle for a day or two from Crane Lake to the Lac la Croix Ranger Station. The hamlet of Crane Lake is north of Duluth, Minnesota, and is reached by driving up Highway 53 to the town of Orr, then turning right onto Highway 24. It can also be reached from the town of Ely by driving west along Echo Trail Road, then a right onto Highway 24.

The ranger station is on the north shore of Lac la Croix, in a sheltered bay east

Girls from Camp Widjiwagan stop for a leech-check while wading Poohbah Creek.

of the village of Lac la Croix and west of Indian Island. The original station was constructed below Twin Falls, on the Maligne River, but was relocated here in 1998 in hopes of providing economic benefits to the Native community. For that same reason, you will also see motorboats here and on many of the neighboring park lakes.

The agreement allowing Native guides to use 10-horsepower motors and to land floatplanes within the park, and to provide increased unemployment aid to the Neguaguon Reserve, was announced in 1993. An overall motorboat ban had been placed on Quetico in 1973. Members of the Lac la Croix Guiding Association were exempt from this regulation for certain lakes (Quetico, Beaverhouse, Wolseley, Tanner, Minn, McAree, French and Pickerel). The 1993 amendment added six more lakes, including Poohbah. The decision to alter the management plan didn't happen overnight, and definitely wasn't made without controversy. Issues between the Lac la Croix people and the park have been going on since Quetico was established. Up until the 1940s local Natives were strongly discouraged from "using" the protected land, with one of the first arrests and evictions of Native "poachers" being on Poohbah Lake. Ironically, the Natives who were apprehended by the first park rangers, Bob Readman and Ephram Crawford, in the fall of 1909 didn't even know the reserve had been established.

Relationships between the opposing groups improved slowly. In 1991 the Minister of Natural Resources, Bud Wildman, even made a formal apology to the Lac la Croix band in the Ontario Legislature for the government's past actions.

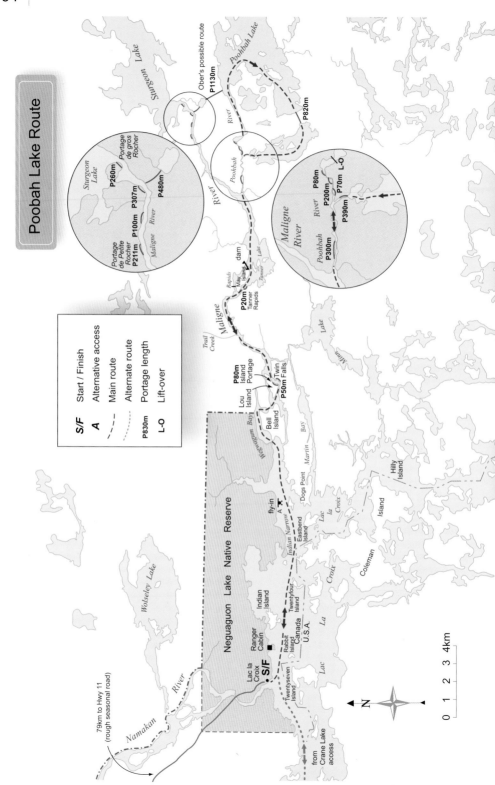

Poobah Lake Route

Sturgeon Lake

Ober's possible route
P1130m

Poohbah Lake

River

P820m

Sturgeon Lake

Portage de gros Rocher
P260m
P307m
P100m
P480m
Maligne River
Portage de Petite Rocher
P211m

Poohbah River

P80m
P200m
P70m L-O
P390m
Maligne River
Poohbah River
P300m

River
Poohbah

Rapids
Maligne
Bay Island dam
Tanner Lake
P20m
Tanner Rapids

Trail Creek

Legend

S/F	Start / Finish
A	Alternative access
– – –	Main route
· · · ·	Alternate route
P830m	Portage length
L-O	Lift-over

P80m Island Portage
Twin Falls
P50m Falls

Lou Island

Bell Island

Weweogun Bay

Neguaguon Lake Native Reserve

fly-in
A

Dogs Point
Martin Bay

Minn Lake
Lac la Croix

Eastbend Island

Hilly Island

Island

Coleman

Indian Narrows

Indian Island

Twentyfour Island

Rabbit Island
Canada
U.S.A.

Ranger Cabin
Lac la Croix
S/F

Twentyseven Island

Lac La Croix

Wolseley Lake

Namakan River

79km to Hwy 11 (rough seasonal road)

from Crane Lake access

N

0 1 2 3 4km

However, major environmental groups working to protect Quetico are still strongly opposed to the motorboats, claiming there should be no compromise when it comes to the preservation of wilderness. Native leaders argue that the elimination of motorboats would be against aboriginal rights and treaty provisions protected by the Canadian constitution.

I can't help wonder what Oberholtzer would think of all this. A good portion of his trip here was motivated by a desire to preserve Native culture and traditional ways. At the time, the Ojibwe respected him more then any other white person, and in turn he respected their traditional ways: "We have so much to learn from Indians and no better place to learn it today than portages worn smooth by our Indian predecessors."

But are motorboats "traditional"? Why not guide from a canoe? On my last trip through the northwest portion of the park, I asked that very question of one of the band members. The answer I got was simple: "Tradition defines my lifestyle but not my mode of travel." He had a point. The majority of guides in Lac la Croix have lost the skill to paddle and portage a canoe because the motorboat made the canoe obsolete many years ago. Living in a remote village, situated on a very large body of water, the motorboat made more sense. When the band member asked me if I was willing to give up my mode of transportation back home in the city for my ancestors' "traditional" ways, the issue became even more complex.

In real terms, however, the moment you begin paddling up the Maligne River the issue over the motorboats becomes quite moot. (The hydro-electric dam the Natives are now planning to build on the Namakan River is a much bigger issue in my opinion.) It's rare to even see a motorboat, and if you do, it takes little away from paddling one of the most scenic waterways in all of Quetico; a characteristic

Maligne River's Tanner Rapids.

that becomes apparent the moment you reach the first obstacle — Twin Falls.

To reach Twin Falls from the northwest corner of Lac la Croix you have a choice between two inlets: a narrow fjord to the right of Bell Island and what's called Wegwaquin Bay, which is to the left of Bell Island. I'd choose the left. That way you can keep close to the lesser exposed northern shore of Lac la Croix after leaving the ranger station.

Twin Falls, located on the southeast side of Lou Island has two portages; one is on the left and another to the right. Even though the route on the left, which avoids the cascade to the left, has a slightly longer 16-rod (88 yd/80 m) portage, it's the one that's regularly used.

Making your way between Twin Falls and Tanner Rapids you'll feel the pull of the current at times, especially where the river narrows somewhat. There are also some marshy bits where in lower water you may have a beaver dam or two to liftover. In higher water levels you also might have to get out wade or line some fast sections. The current is especially strong halfway between Twin Falls and the entrance of Trail Creek (east of Trail Creek look for the remains of an old logging site) as well as where the river empties out of the channel on the north side of May Island. But there are no real difficult spots. Even the next portage, found on the south channel of May Island and to the right of Tanner Rapids, measures only 4 rods (22 yd/20 m) (for the history of Tanner Rapids see the Hunter Island chapter).

Tanner is the next lake en route, and if you haven't stopped to camp at the small island sites above Twin Falls, then the islands above Tanner Rapids are the place to stay. This area is different from the rest of Quetico. The lake is shallow with dark, murky water. The shoreline has a few pines, patches of cedar and gnarled birch trees. Nothing really special, I guess, but the rock formations set it apart. I know little about geology, but these slabs of what I think is a type of meta-morphic rock, and what is noted in the Quetico Foundation's 1959 guidebook as "rocks that have weathered to an unusual wart-like appearance," are undeniably bizarre looking and definitely worth stopping to look at.

Bald eagle sightings are becoming an increasingly common occurrence in Quetico.

Legendary canoeist Bill Mason paddled up the Maligne River from Tanner Lake in 1956 while working for filmmaker Chris Chapman. The Quetico Foundation hired Chapman to produce a film entitled *Quetico* and chose a young Bill Mason to be the guide, cook and "actor" in the film. Chapman recalled meeting his assistant: "I knocked on the door of this house; the door opened, I didn't see anybody! I looked down, and there was this BOY!

Waiting for the morning mist to rise on Tanner Lake.

And I thought — I was expecting some old trapper-canoeists that I was going to put in my film! Well, this guy was so enthusiastic; he was so excited and so I thought, 'There's nothing I can do but have him along.'"

Chapman and Mason spent a good portion of their three-week trip in Quetico filming on the Maligne, capturing scenes of portaging and running the upper rapids. Mason was ecstatic about the project, so much so he decided shortly after the trip to change his career from commercial artist to filmmaker. By 1959 he had started work on his first motion picture, *Wilderness Treasures*, filmed at a summer camp in nearby Lake of the Woods. From there, he continued to make films (*Paddle to the Sea, Cry of the Wild, Song of the Paddle, Waterwalker*) and quickly became one of the most notable documentary filmmakers, canoeists and environmentalists of his time. Throughout Mason's career, "the guy in the red canoe" that he portrayed in Chapman's *Quetico* continued to be the essential character in his own award-winning films.

I wonder if Bill Mason knew back then, while paddling on the Maligne River with Chapman, how the "red canoe" symbol would come to represent the freedom of wilderness travel.

The creek leading to Poohbah Lake is not far upstream from Tanner and is partially hidden by a giant patch of sedge grass and horsetails. The route up the creek is shallow, rocky and comes with four short-but-rough portages. But it's a lot easier than the way Oberholtzer and Magee went. Ober's journal entries and photos taken en route suggest they portaged to Poohbah further up the Maligne River, somewhere past the second rapids down from Sturgeon Lake. I'm not exactly sure where from, though. The only alternative route to Poohbah from the top end of Maligne is from a very overgrown portage near the base of the second rapid. My regular canoe companion, Andy Baxter, and I tried it out the first time we went into Poohbah and found it resembled a moose trail more than an actual portage. The trail was marked on our U.S. McKenzie Map, but I have my doubts that it's even used by modern-day canoeists. In fact, I suspect few even know it exists. To use the trail we first had to make our way up the Maligne River, which is no easy task once you pass the mouth of Poohbah Creek. Then the beginning of the portage was nearly impossible to find, and even when we began walking it, we went past our knees in pools of muck. About a quarter of the way along, we paddled over a small lake — more of a bog by the end — and waded through a couple more swamps before finding Poohbah. The distance totaled 320 rods (1,760 yd/1610 m). Believe me, the creek is far easier.

The initial stretch of Poohbah Creek is shallow, and there's no true route to follow except straight through the tufts of marsh grass. But not too far upstream is the first of four portages, found to the left and avoiding two consecutive logging dams made out of large boulders. The trail measures less than 60 rods (330 yd/300 m) and is flat but muddy in sections. The water route twists through a wide, marshy area alive with duck, heron, osprey, mink, otter and one of the largest populations of dragonflies and damselflies I've ever seen in my life. The creek eventually splits. To the right, a 78-rod (429 yd/390 m) portage heads into Wink Lake (another alternative way in to Poohbah); and to the left there's a 14-rod (77 yd/70 m) portage marked on the right of a small rapid, thus avoiding another boulder dam. Take the route to the left. The trail begins a few yards up from the base of the rapid, but it's far better for your canoe if you get out directly at the rapids and walk up to the trail. For the same reason, it's better to follow the portage all the way to the end.

The third portage, measuring around 40 rods (220 yd/200 m), isn't too far upstream from the second. Keep to the main part of the creek, heading up a shallow, rocky stretch where you have to pass under a downed tree. The trail is to the left and keeps fairly close to the creek, especially during the last quarter. Around the next bend is the fourth and final portage. It's a rough 15-rod (83 yd/80 m) trail on the left-hand side of a rock-strewn rapid. It's possible to line up this section of quick water, however, avoiding the portage all together.

Poohbah is to the right of the last rapid, but there's still a long, narrow section complete with a shallow stretch that you may have to lift over or wade through. However, the moment the waterway opens up and you get a glimpse across the expanse of Poohbah, you'll realize why Oberholtzer listed it as his favorite lake: "September 6, 1909: Reached Poohbah Lake at half past six and was tired. Fortunately we had a perfect day and we now had a perfectly clear night with the sky abloom with stars. They made a good deal of light and some of them threw long spiral reflections upon the water. I had to finish pitching the

Another great bush meal on Poohbah Lake.

tent in the dark on site of a large old Indian wigwam. Billy said the Indians had been making canoes there and it was a favorite lake for that purpose." (The Native name for the lake is *Gan dook gwe ma*, which means "place for getting bark canoes." Poohbah is taken from a character in Gilbert and Sullivan's 1885 opera hit, *The Mikado*.)

This truly is an amazing place, with islands of stunted pine and rocky shoals. Many canoeists also consider it the centerpiece of Quetico, not necessarily for the location but because of the difficulty getting there. Routes from the east and south are even more of an inconvenience, which is probably why the fishing is so exceptional. The lake holds lake trout, smallmouth bass, walleye and monster northern pike.

When we first came to Poohbah from the north, we cast our lures out the moment we reached the lake, and in less then a minute Andy hooked into a pike. He fought it for a good 15 minutes before we got a glimpse of the fish. Its overall girth was more impressive than its length, even though it measured over half the size of our 17-foot canoe. I swear the pike was so old it had moss growing on its head. We were terrified of the thing. I was the one elected to release it. There was no way I was going to attempt lifting it into the canoe. That would have been a disaster for sure. Instead, I pulled the lure out of its gaping jaws with a pair of pliers, praying the entire time that my hand wouldn't get bitten or caught in the lure's hooks. The beast was eventually released without mishap, but we made a pact to forgo our evening swim.

Spend two or three days exploring Poohbah before backtracking to Lac la Croix. It's also a good idea to leave via the alternative route through Wink Lake, though it's not an easy way out. The portage linking Poohbah's eastern bay with Wink measures 163 rods (897 yd/820 m). It begins with an abrupt uphill battle and ends with an insanely long, steep downhill grade. The 78-rod (429 yd/390 m) portage that leads from the southern end of Wink to Poohbah Creek is also difficult. You travel up and over a knoll and then through knee-deep muck. And you still have to carry over the first portage that took you into the creek from the Maligne River. But like Poohbah, Wink Lake is extremely scenic and the fishing is phenomenal.

The Poohbah route is definitely a challenge at times, and the majority of paddlers simply stay put somewhere along the Maligne River, but a trip in and out of Poohbah will inspire you to search out even more wild places, just as it did for Oberholtzer and Magee. In 1912 they paddled from Winnipeg to Hudson Bay and back, a 2,000-mile (3,220 km) trek lasting 144 days, a time spent in the wilderness that Oberholtzer labeled the single most powerful experience of his life. Afterwards he became a top conservationist and, more importantly, a leader in the development the 10-million-acre Quetico-Superior region.

Your trip to Poohbah may or may not be as influential to you, but at least Andy's big pike awaits recapture.

Poohbah Lake Route

LENGTH: 5–6 days

PORTAGES: 11

LONGEST PORTAGE: 163 rods (897 yd/820 m)

DIFFICULTY: Intermediate canoe-tripping skills are required.

ACCESS: To reach the Native Reserve and ranger station of Lac la Croix, continue past the second fork on the Beaverhouse Lake access road. The total distance once you turn south off Highway 11 is 50 miles (79 km). This is a rough, seasonally maintained road, so make sure to phone the park to ask about conditions prior to your trip. Parking and a canoe launch are available in the small town of Lac la Croix, and the ranger station is located in a small bay along the north shore about a half-hour paddle from town.

ALTERNATIVE ACCESS: Many paddlers book a shuttle boat from Crane Lake access or a bushplane flight from outfitters either outside of Atikokan or Ely (boats and planes are allowed to land on Lac la Croix, close to the mouth of the Maligne River). Some canoeists even paddle for a day or two from Crane Lake to the Lac la Croix Ranger Station. The hamlet of Crane Lake is north of Duluth, Minnesota, and is reached by driving up Highway 53 to the town of Orr, then turning right onto Highway 24. It can also be reached from the town of Ely by driving west along Echo Trail Road, then right onto Highway 24.

TOPOGRAPHICAL MAPS: 52-B/15, 52-C/8

FISHER MAPS: F-23, F-24

7 Bentpine Creek Loop

I DOUBT THERE'S A SINGLE PADDLER who's not thankful that logging in Quetico was stopped back in 1971. At the same time, many of us feel some sense of admiration for the loggers themselves. Timbermen have always had a culture all to their own, especially in the era prior to mechanization. There was a romance to the loggers' life, an appreciation for the hardships of living and working in the bush. Loggers had their own customs, songs, tall tales, even their own dialect. Eventually the ring of the axe fell silent beneath the din of motorized saws and cutters, horse-drawn sleighs were replaced by diesel trucks, and lumber barons, often with short-sighted economics, political sponsorship and motivated by just plain gluttony, took all the romance away.

For canoeists who wish to visit this lost era and see remnants of old lumber camps where the songs were sung and the tall tales told, and also to witness where the resilient forests have regrown, there's no better place than the Bentpine Creek watershed in Quetico's northwest corner.

The route begins at Beaverhouse Lake, which is reached by driving west for 24 miles (39 km) from Atikokan on Highway 11 then south on the dirt road opposite Flanders Road (look for the park sign). It is 14 miles (22 km) to the parking area. The road is gravel but well maintained until where it forks at the 9-mile (15 km) mark. Take the left fork here. The remaining way is a rough, much smaller roadway. Make sure you contact the park prior to your trip and ask about conditions. To reach the lake, you have to portage straight south from the parking area for 120 rods (660 yd/600 m).

All of the large lakes in Quetico can become problematic in high winds, but Beaverhouse has to be the worst. It's not the size of the lake that's an issue, really. It's where you have to travel on it. The route between the access point and the ranger station follows the eastern portion of the lake, heading from north to south. The wind generally blows from the west, and this can make for dangerous paddling conditions.

Andy Baxter and I chose this route for our trip in 2006. We had just finished a 14-day trip in the east end of the park and had no issues with wind the entire time we were out. The moment we began our way across Beaverhouse, however, the winds rose, and we found ourselves stuck on a large island halfway to the ranger station.

There's a real danger of becoming windbound early in your trip. You're usually so excited about finally being able to go paddling that there's a tendency to ignore logic and attempt to make it through the heavy chop. It happened to Andy and me. The entire time we waited for the wind to die down, we fought the urge

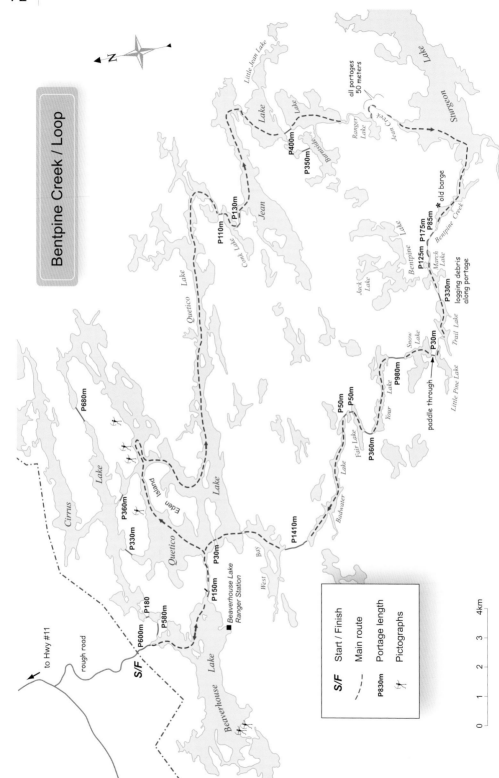

Bentpine Creek / Loop

to Hwy #11

rough road

S/F

P600m
P580m
P180
P150m
P30m
P330m
P360m
P330m
P680m

Beaverhouse Lake Ranger Station

West Bay

Beaverhouse Lake

Cirrus Lake

Eden Island

Quetico Lake

Quetico Lake

P1410m

P50m P50m
P360m

Fair Lake
Budwater Lake

Your Lake

Snow Lake
P980m
P30m

paddle through

Little Pine Lake

Trail Lake

P330m
logging debris along portage

March Lake

P125m P175m
P85m
Bentpine

Jack Lake

Bentpine Creek

* old barge

Conk Lake

P110m P130m

Jean Lake

Little Jean Lake

Lake

Lake

P400m
P350m

Banmashie

Ranger Lake

Jean Creek

Sturgeon Lake

all portages 50 meters

Legend

S/F Start / Finish

- - - Main route

P830m Portage length

✈ Pictographs

0 1 2 3 4km

Boys from Camp Widjiwagan having the adventure of a lifetime on Fair Lake.

to paddle. And we weren't alone. Two other parties joined us on the island. A third group passed us and headed blindly out across the center of the bay, and soon paid the consequences. Almost immediately they were broadsided by a large swell and flipped over. None of us could help them from where we were. We could only watch as they drifted with the wind, desperately holding onto their over-turned canoe. Ten minutes into the ordeal, a rescue was attempted by the ranger from the nearby station. We watched as he tried to maneuver his motorboat towards them, but even he couldn't manage the waves.

Thankfully they reached the opposite shoreline about half an hour later. We watched through binoculars as they dragged their sodden bodies up on the beach site like a pair of drowned rats.

By 6:00 P.M. the wind had calmed enough for us to safely cross over to the ranger station and check in, then paddle over to camp where the Quetico River flushes into Beaverhouse Lake. Along the way, we took time to visit the canoeists who had flipped over earlier on. Other then their pride, the only injuries were a few bruises to their legs and arms, caused by holding onto the canoe and being tossed about in the waves. Their gear had got the worst of it. Everything except for a few necessities, a tent and sleeping bags, had been lost. They were forced to call it quits. How ironic that a trip they had planned for months was over simply because they were in a rush to begin it.

In the morning we only had to paddle ten minutes up the Quetico River from our campsite to reach the first portage. The 30-rod (165 yd/150 m) trail is to the right of a moderate cascade and offers a good display of logging relics. There's a short swift prior the takeout, which we decided to paddle up. It might have been a better idea to wade or line the canoe, however. Halfway up we noticed bits and pieces of camping gear resting on the bottom, an obvious sign that some canoes hadn't made it.

There are two possible takeouts after the swift. Both lead you up the steep riverbank and through a large field cluttered with the remains of a lumber camp. Taking the second allows you a closer look at an old logging chute rotting close to the shoreline.

A lot of wood went through here. In 1918 four million board feet of pine were cut out of Quetico and Beaverhouse Lakes, 26 million the following year — and the logging camp was just one of five established by the Shelvin-Clark company in the area.

After the put-in Andy and I continued up the Quetico River for a half-hour or so, with the waterway becoming wider the closer it came to Quetico Lake. From here our route was directly to the east, keeping close to the south shore. The north shore, however, holds a major display of pictographs, and we couldn't pass up the chance to check them out. We took the long way around Quetico Lake, hoping the morning calm would continue long enough for us to visit the Native paintings.

What an incredible place! The north shore holds four amazing clusters of paintings. The first group is located directly north of Eden Island, above a large pile of boulders. The site consists mainly of a circular disk surrounded by hand-prints. The symbols themselves aren't as clear as those at other sites, but what they represent is really quite unique. The disk is thought to be a shield, and the handprints encircling it signifies the coming of war. Alternatively, the disk is the door to the spirit world, with the handprints having been left behind as a taunt-ing gesture by the mischievous Maymaygwayshiuk.

The next three pictograph sites are found further to the east along the north-ern arm of Quetico Lake. The first is made up of a line of dots, representing the path taken by the artist on his journey of becoming a shaman; the second is a series of zigzag lines and what appears to be, to me anyway, the head of a cow moose. The last site, which I'd consider to be one of the most striking in all of Quetico Park, features a large group of images: a moose, caribou, a large vertical line, two crosses, two Maymaygwayshi (one with an erect penis), and two canoes, a small one with two occupants and a larger one with six paddlers, one standing up with his arms reaching towards the sky.

We spent a good two hours checking out the pictographs, and then paddled back south to Quetico's eastern inlet. From there, we still had another 7 miles (12 km) to go to reach the end of the lake. With only a slight breeze blowing from the

The north shore of Quetico Lake holds four amazing clusters of Native pictographs.

west, conditions were perfect to sail our canoe. By mid-afternoon we had reached the far end of Quetico Lake, where we had intended on camping. With extra time on our hands, however, we decided to continue south and take on the two portages, 22 rods (120 yd/110 m) and 25 rods (137 yd/130 m), in to Jean Lake before calling it a day.

The first carry was a short but relatively steep portage located in the corner of the southern bay. The takeout is to the extreme right of a 30-foot (10 m) cascade gushing out of Conk Lake. And the second is an even easier trail located almost directly across Conk Lake. Both portages have logging artifacts to check out, and it was at the put-in on Jean Lake that the first timber cruiser, L.W. Ayer, who was sent out in 1903 to what is now Quetico, wrote in his journal: "The timber is at this point the best I have seen in Canada. It is 25% white pine, 46% Norway [red pine]." After that statement, the race was on. By 1904 the Rainy River Lumber Company had begun operations, and in less than six years it split into several competitors, the largest being Shelvin-Clark. By 1954 that company alone had processed 800 million board feet of lumber.

The decision to camp on Jean Lake made for a long day. Andy and I had paddled 24 miles (39 km) in total. However, as we sat around the fire that evening recounting the day's events, we could only think of one awkward moment during the day: when we were attacked by a beaver. It had happened while we were checking out the Native pictographs. We were making our way quietly around each bend, carefully searching the rock ledges for the next set of paintings, when

An old barge from the logging era marks the entrance to Bentpine Creek.

we surprised a beaver sunning itself atop a boulder. We were less then a paddle's length away from the poor beast when we startled it. Scared silly, the large rodent reacted by leaping into the air then scrambling towards the water. On the way down, he managed to lose his footing, trip head over heels and land smack dab on our packs, loaded in the center of the canoe. Andy and I just sat there dumbfounded as the beaver hissed and snapped its teeth at us before diving into the water, never to be seen again.

Other than the beaver encounter, our second day out was a great success. Our third day was even better. The 80-rod (440 yd/400 m) portage over from the south end of Jean to Burntside Lake was an easy walk, except for a slightly muddy section near the end, and we got to check out the remains of the ranger's cabin close to the put-in. After Rouge Lake, the next four portages, all found to the left along Jean Creek, measured no more than 10 rods (55 yd/50 m), and due to high water the last one wasn't even necessary. Sturgeon Lake was also surprisingly calm, and it took us only until noon to paddle near the entrance to the northwestern inlet, which leads up to Bentpine Creek.

Once again we altered our camping plans. The islands on the west end of Sturgeon were to have been our original stopover sites for day three. However, we noticed that over half the campsites were already taken, so we opted to continue up Bentpine. Crowds would definitely not be an issue here. And besides, the trip really didn't get started for us until we reached Bentpine Creek. This was new territory for both of us, and we were looking forward to finding more logging-era relics. Bentpine Creek houses some of the best in the park.

Not far from the first portage was an old barge pushed up along the eastern shoreline, and to the left of the takeout were the ruins of a third logging chute. Both date back to the late 1930s.

The trail, found to the right of the creek, measures only 17 rods (93 yd/85 m) and leads up a slight incline. Due to its lack of use, however, it has a few drawbacks. The takeout was in a mud hole, and the whereabouts of the put-in was questionable at best (we ended up finding it to the right of a rock ledge). Giant patches of poison ivy also grew thick along its edges. And worst of all were the dozen or so ticks that grabbed onto our pant legs as we walked through.

The next portage was better. It measured 35 rods (192 yd/175 m). And a third, almost directly after the second, measured 25 rods (137 yd/125 m). Both had more logging artifacts to check out. But they were cursed with muddy takeouts — and more ticks! We had performed a tick check at the end of each previous portage and found none seriously attached to our clothes. Just as we were about to push off from the third carry, however, I felt a tickle on my left thigh. Lifting my pant leg I discovered four had embedded themselves in my skin. Andy then checked himself and found three.

We tried not to panic. If you yank them out, you're liable to pull them in half, leaving the head inside your skin and increasing the chance of infection. Staying relatively calm, Andy sprayed a good dose of bug repellent on the exposed tick to make it relax its grip (it actually breaths out of its butt while its head is lodged in your skin). Then, after allowing some time for the repellent to kick in, he took hold of each of the parasites in turn with a pair of tweezers, and, without squeezing, gently pulled each one out. It was my turn. I reached over to grab the tweezers from Andy and suddenly felt another tickle, this time under my private parts. Complete hysteria set in! I pulled my trousers down, reached under my apparatus, and yanked the tick away.

The pain wasn't immediate, but eventually there was uncontrollable burning and itching at the spot where the tick had plunged its sharp mouthpart deep inside me and secreted its cement-like salvia to glue itself in place. My first-aid manual said to have someone check the bitten area (ticks are known vectors of Lyme disease), but Andy would have nothing to do with it, so I resorted to using my compass mirror. I gingerly applied some ointment to the growing rash and used my lifejacket as a seat cushion for the remainder of the trip.

Before calling it a day on Trail Lake, we first had to paddle across a widening in the creek and then portage 60 rods (330 yd/300 m) up and over a moderate slope. To the left side of the last portage, leading into Trail Lake, we found a run of steel rollers that had been used to haul logs overland. The system was built from Trail Lake to March Lake by J.A. Mathieu of Shelvin-Clarke Company in 1936 and was the longest ever used. It's impressive, to say the least, but technology such as this also marked the beginning of the end for the lumbermen. Close to 50 million board feet were cut and hauled out of here by Shelvin-Clarke.

The story of Shelvin-Clarke and the Quetico forest is so similar to Dr. Seuss's book *The Lorax*, it's frightening. As early as 1917 the company was known for its over-the-top logging practices. A deal with the Minister of Lands and Forests to pay half the market value for 13,340 acres (5400 hectares) of Quetico forest created one of the greatest scandals in Ontario provincial politics. By 1936 even the company's workers questioned their employer's motives and went on strike. Mathieu and other northern timber barons were quickly losing face.

Conservationists then had to move quickly to save what was left of the forest. In 1941 a new park superintendent was appointed, Frank MacDougall, the first ever to make logging second to tourism as a park priority. Three decades later, in 1970, the Quetico Park Advisory Committee held public meetings regarding the future of logging in the park and came up with this definition of how Quetico should be managed: "...it's preservation, in perpetuity, for the people of Ontario as an area of wilderness not adversely affected by human activities and containing a natural environment of aesthetic, historical and recreational significance." A year later, logging was banned from the park.

Day four of our trip was the shortest distance we paddled overall, and again we made camp that night at a spot other than the one in our original plan. We figured we'd push all the way to Quetico Lake, but we only made it to Badwater Lake. We hadn't even considered camping on this lake prior to the trip, first because of the name (the early loggers reported it to have bad-tasting water) and

second because other canoeists told us that it had no campsites. In fact, we were told by the same canoeists that the portages between Trail and Badwater Lakes were unmanageable and that the lakes in between weren't even worth visiting. These accounts were completely inaccurate, of course.

First off, the portages from Trail to Badwater were much easier then we thought. The first, a 5-rod (27 yd/30 m) portage from Little Pine Lake to Snow Lake (found to the left of a small swift shortly after the navigable stream takes you out of Trail Lake), wasn't even necessary. We just pad-

Running low on T.P. supplies is a sure sign the trip is coming to an end. Andy Baxter, Badwater Lake.

There's nothing better then sipping on a bush martini after a long day of portaging.

dled through. The 195-rod (1,072 yd/980 m) portage from the northeast corner of Snow Lake to Your Lake wasn't what we thought either. It was certainly a long haul, with two small hills and one medium-sized mud hole in between. Overall, though, it wasn't a bad carry, and there were some impressive old cedar trees to gawk at along the way. The third portage, linking the far northwest end of Your Lake to Fair Lake, was also a couple hundred yards shorter than what our map indicated. Mind you, its exact whereabouts was confusing at first. Andy and I attempted to paddle up the creek and were forced to turn back after spotting three massive beaver dams blocking the way. We then found a false trail on the left side of the creek that led to nowhere in particular. Finally, to the far left of the creek, we discovered an actual 30-rod (165 yd/150 m) portage linking us to a small pond that connects to the south end of Fair Lake. And the two remaining portages, taking us in and out of another pond before reaching Badwater Lake, measured less than 20 rods (110 yd/100 m). The first, located at the far eastern end of Fair, went up and over a small knoll, and the second crossed a creek near the takeout and over a boggy area near the put-in.

The claims that Badwater Lake had no campsites were completely untrue. There are at least eight prime spots to pitch a tent. Andy and I took the first one we spotted, located on an island just past the portage, because we thought it would be the only campsite on the lake. By doing so, we had ended our day early.

Park regulars end another successful misadventure in the park at Beaverhouse Lake access.

But that was okay; Badwater was an excellent spot to hang out. We caught wall-eye, pike and lake trout not far from the island. A bald eagle gave us a visit just before super. Three otters walked past our beached canoe, with one stopping to give it a sniff. Behind our tent, Andy was chased by a mother grouse protecting her nest (I'd never heard a grouse hiss at someone before). And a painted turtle surprised us by walking straight out of the water and over to the fire pit where we were sitting. I guess it's true — beauty is in the eye of the beholder. This was the best stopover we had during the entire trip.

Badwater Lake stretches out to almost 5 miles (8 km) in length. It took us most of the morning to reach the portage at the far end, then most of the afternoon to carry over the 280 rods (1,540 yd/1410 m) to Quetico Lake's west bay. The same group of canoeists who alleged that the previous portages were tough and that Badwater Lake had no campsites also reported that the portage out of Badwater was absolutely horrible. They were right this time. But that was only because the maintenance crew hadn't been in yet that year to clear out some fallen trees. The hills they told us about didn't exist, and the two swamps along the way had logs placed to make walking across the muddy spots more manageable. Still, we were pretty tired by the end of it, and to make matters worse a strong north-west wind was blowing across Quetico Lake when we arrived.

Andy and I were able to paddle across the west bay, but when we carried over the 5-rod (27 yd/25 m) portage linking the bay with the rest of Quetico Lake, the conditions were far too rough for us to continue on. The wind was so severe at this point (we later found out that the area had received tornado warnings) that a row of whitecaps had formed all the way across to the mouth of the Quetico River. This was to be our route for the rest of the day, back to familiar Beaverhouse Lake (by way of the 30 rod/165 yd/150 m portage) to make camp on the same site we had stayed on the first night. One look at the brutal waves out on the lake, however, and we knew that reaching Beaverhouse was definitely not going to happen. So, once again we altered our plans (we were quite used to it by this point) and set up our tent directly on the put-in of the 5-rod (27 yd/25 m) portage.

It was an ideal spot to camp our last evening out really. There was a gorgeous sandy beach and a fire pit tucked away in the backwoods, well protected from the heavy gusts of wind. But that wasn't the main reason. Quetico Lake was much more fitting than Beaverhouse because of its name. Three reasons are given to how as it got labeled in the first place, and all three have some significance to our journey. The first is that the word "Quetico" is a short term for the Quebec Timber Company; the second is that Quetico is an Ojibwe word for "bad," "dangerous," "a place where it's better to paddle along the shore because of high winds;" and the third is from an older Ojibwe word, one with mythological connotations, a label given to a place holding some type of "benevolent spirit."

Of the three definitions, the third is the least likely to be true. However, it was the one we chose to believe in. This area we had just paddled, as with the rest of Quetico Park, undeniably deserves such a strong and beautiful description.

Bentpine Creek Loop

LENGTH: 5–6 days

PORTAGES: 18

LONGEST PORTAGE:
280 rods (1,540 yd/1410 m)

DIFFICULTY: Advanced novice to intermediate canoe-tripping skills are required.

ACCESS: Beaverhouse Lake is reached by driving west from Atikokan on Highway 11 for 24 miles (39 km), then turn south on the dirt road opposite of Flanders Road (look for the park sign). It's 14 miles (22 km) to the parking area. The road is gravel but well maintained until where it forks at the 9-mile (15 km) mark. Take the left fork here. The remaining way is rough and a much smaller roadway. Make sure you contact the park prior to your trip and ask about conditions. From the parking area you have to portage straight south for 120 rods (660 yd/ 600 m) to reach the lake. The ranger station is situated on a small, deep southeast bay of Beaverhouse Lake.

ALTERNATIVE ACCESS: It's possible for outfitters from Crane Lake or Ely to fly you in to Beaverhouse Lake.

TOPOGRAPHICAL MAPS:
52-B/5, 52-B/12, 52-C/12

FISHER MAPS: F-23, F-24, F-28

Pitcher Plant in full bloom.

8 Wawiag River Loop

FORTUNATELY I WASN'T GOING TOP SPEED on the highway when the bolts came off of my front wheel. The teenagers who thought it was cool to loosen the wheel bolts on a stranger's truck under the cover of darkness were caught and convicted after being ratted out by a friend when another victim was seriously injured (three other vehicles were violated on the street that night). But they never did fulfill their sentence in juvenile detention, and they were back pulling pranks again in less than two months. The police's response to all the victims was that we just happened to be in the wrong place at the wrong time. They were right about that. I decided to get out of town to someplace safer — I went canoeing in Quetico.

I chose a route through a remote part of the park, a six-day loop in the Wawiag River system. However, to begin the trip I had to launch from one of the busiest lakes in the park, Saganaga Lake. This body of water is situated in the southeast end of Quetico and is in no way isolated from the social woes of our modern world. It's busy with motorboats, lodges and frantic canoeists racing across to reach more out-of-the way places.

Don't get me wrong, it's still a scenic spot, but paddling across Saganaga Lake can be depressing, especially if you've happened to read Sigurd Olson's essay *Farewell to Saganaga*. It tells the story of how he revisits his favorite wilderness lake only to discover it has been plagued by development. His story reveals the struggle between the goodness one can still find in human companionship and the evils of modernization (though there's no mention of teenagers loosening strangers' wheels).

Like Olson, I escaped the busyness of Saganaga by heading north toward Cache Bay. I took the water taxi. Olson would not have approved of my choice of transportation, but in my opinion the damage of encroachment is already done here, and the shuttle turned an all-day paddle across a large and somewhat urbanized lake into a 20-minute boat ride.

After being dropped off by the boat shuttle at Hook Island (they can't go any further), I paddled over to the ranger station to pick up my permit. Then I camped my first night just north on a small, rocky outcrop. It wasn't even a designated site, just enough space back in the bush to pitch my tent on, and a nice slab of granite along the shoreline where I could sit and watch the sunset.

From Cache Bay the route heads to Saganagons Lake, with two route choices: a chain of small lakes linked by short portages, beginning on the northern-most inlet of Cache Bay, and a 140-rod (770 yd/700 m) portage to the right of Silver Falls, located in the northwestern inlet of Cache Bay. The first option is rarely used and was my original route plan, but I also desperately wanted to view the cascade, so I carried around Silver Falls instead.

The trail heads downhill most of the way and isn't too bad as long as you're going from Cache Bay to Saganagons and not vice versa. I ended up trying a short-cut leading to the rapids at the base of the falls but ended up walking most of the stream, constantly unloading and loading the canoe. It's far better to keep to the main path all the way along.

Saganagons Lake was pretty much free of canoeists the moment I paddled east, past the route which heads to the popular Falls Chain. I took my time here, spending most of the day making my way down to the far end of the lake. At noon I stopped for a shore lunch of walleye fillets and during mid-afternoon found time to explore the remains of the Powell Homestead.

The old farm is at the head of Saganagons Lake, and it was here that Jack Powell, a logger from Basswood Lake, and wife, Mary Ottertail, an Ojibwe from Lac la Croix, settled after being married in 1901. Life was spent growing vegetables, mostly potatoes planted on the nearby islands where the soil was suitable for them to take root, and trapping. They gathered wild rice, boiled birch sap, picked blueberries, went to town twice a year for supplies, and once even hauled a cow back with them on a wooden scow, towed by a canoe and two outboard motors lashed to either side.

The Powell family left in 1954 to live at Saganaga. During their half-century of full-time existence here, five children were born and three grandchildren were raised. Their first son, Bill, eventually opened up a resort on Saganaga Lake, which could very well be the same place Olson wrote about in *Farewell to Saganaga* (how ironic that would be, since the Powells' homestead was the last year-round residence to be allowed in Quetico park). The second son, Mike, worked as a fire ranger in Quetico with his father in the 1920s. The third son, Frank, taught himself to fly a bushplane. Daughters Esther and Tempest continued to live a life of trapping and guiding. And granddaughter Betty Powell Skoog ended up writing an incredible account of the life on Saganagons Lake, entitled *A Life in Two Worlds*. Betty returned to the old settlement in 1999 and wrote: "The happiest thing I saw there was when I got out of the canoe and walked up to the cabin and saw that the little creek that ran behind the cabin had been damned up by the beaver. There was now a little pond and there was a beaver house next to the cabin. The first thing I said to the people who went with us was 'Oh look, grandma and grandpa have come back as beaver.' They never wanted to leave Saganagons and they wanted to live their whole lives here and be buried here."

In 1995 almost the entire north shore of Saganagons Lake was burned. In fact, the majority of my chosen route north suffered the same forest fire, which is why many canoeists opt not to go this way anymore. But it's still a strikingly beautiful area, and more importantly, I had it all to myself.

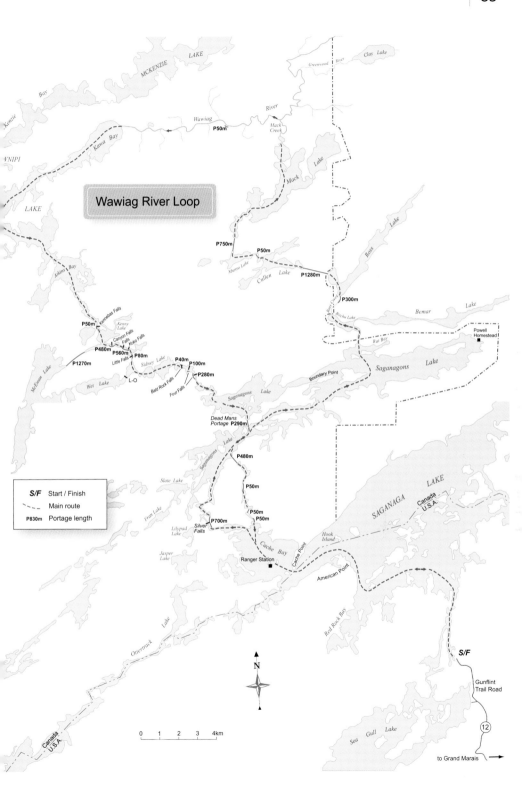

Wawiag River Loop

S/F Start / Finish
- - - Main route
P830m Portage length

P50m
P750m
P50m
P1280m
P300m
P50m
Kennebas Falls
Canyon Falls
Koko Falls
P480m
P560m
P80m
Little Falls
P1270m
P40m
P100m
P280m
Bald Rock Falls
Four Falls
L-O
Dead Mans
Portage P290m
P480m
P50m
P50m
P50m
P700m
Silver
Falls
Ranger Station
Boundary Point
Powell
Homestead

MCKENZIE LAKE
Kenzie Bay
Kawa Bay
VNIPI LAKE
Aikins Bay
Wawiag River
Mack Creek
Mack Lake
Ross Lake
Munro Lake
Cullen Lake
Bitchu Lake
Rat Bay
Bemar Lake
Saganagons Lake
Kenny Lake
McEwan Lake
Wet Lake
Sidney Lake
Saganagons Lake
Slate Lake
Fran Lake
Lilypad Lake
Jasper Lake
Cache Bay
Cache Point
Hook Island
SAGANAGA LAKE
Canada U.S.A.
American Point
Ottertrack Lake
Canada U.S.A.
Red Rock Bay
Greenwood River
Clay Lake

S/F
Gunflint
Trail Road
(12)
to Grand Marais

N

0 1 2 3 4km

From the north shore of Saganagons Lake's Rat Bay, I headed up a twisting creek to Bitchu Lake. My old map indicated a portage here, but I paddled straight through, then took another small creek joining Bitchu to Ross Lake. Just before the creek reaches Ross Lake, there's a 60-rod (330 yd/300 m) portage to the right of the creek, but high water allowed me to paddle most of the way and I only needed to use the last 6 rods (33 yd/30 m) of it.

I considered making an early camp at the southwest end of Ross Lake, but the fire had pretty much eliminated any possible sites. Worst of all, there were boats stashed near the landing and some trash left behind. Since most of Ross lies outside the park boundary and has been scarred not only by fire but also by easy access, I'm reminded that the easier it is to reach a wilderness lake, the less it resembles one when you get there.

Continuing on wasn't a great idea, though. I had to take on a 255-rod (1,400 yd/1280 m) portage linking Ross Lake's northwest bay to Cullen Lake. To find the takeout I had to first push through a marshy section and lift over a fallen tree. Once I got going, however, it wasn't a bad carry. Cullen Lake's eastern narrows also had some greener spots, untouched by the fire, and I was able to pitch my tent away from charred trees and blackened soil.

The morning of day three I was up early, taking on an easy 10-rod (55 yd/50 m) portage located in the northwest inlet of Cullen, south of a creek linking up to Munro Lake; and before stopping for brunch on Mack Lake, I carried across a 150-rod (825 yd/750 m) portage beginning in the northwest corner of Munro. It wasn't a bad carry either, except for the last marshy bit where I had to balance over half submerged logs and rocks to push my canoe out into the open waters of Mack. It's a gorgeous spot.

By reaching Mack Lake midday, I had a decision to make. I could either keep going and hope to find a place to camp along the Wawiag River, or stop early to camp on Mack Lake and take advantage of its notable pike, bass and walleye fishing. I chose to keep going.

The paddling and portaging were easy along Mack Creek, and the waterway opened up a fair bit once I turned left on Wawiag River. At the confluence I met a bunch of anglers rushing downstream to Kawa Bay, the eastern most bay of Kiwnipi Lake. They had come in by floatplane from Clay Lake. It's a common access point for people looking to get into this wilderness area quick and easy. Clay Lake is outside the park boundary, and a couple of outfitters will fly you in. From there, you have to paddle Greenwood Creek. But be warned, this creek is only a few feet wide, full of logjams, and can become unnavigable in low water conditions.

I let the fishermen paddle ahead of me so I could have the river section all to myself. One advantage of the Wawiag is that if you actually do meet someone on it, they are usually in a hurry to reach some other destination. No one seems to

Campsites may be difficult to find in areas that were burned over in 1995, but if you do find one, you're more likely to have the place to yourself.

want to spend time here. For that reason alone, I made camp where a short portage is found to the left of a small set of rapids.

The Wawiag River wasn't always so free of people. In the early 1900s, the Ojibwe of Kawa Bay told park ranger Robert Readman of a trading post that had operated about two and a half miles upriver. Bob Wells, a ranger back in the 1930s, also noted seeing "wigwams" along the river. As a travel route for natives, it was literally a highway, being part of the trail to their "conjuring grounds" on Shebandowan Lake. It was also a well-known route for poachers trying to sneak their fortune in beaver pelts out of the park. But now it's just a weed-choked river that everyone seems to want to avoid. It's strange how our perspectives of the landscape change over time.

The campsite I chose along the Wawiag was probably the only possible stopover on the entire river. I think it also had to be the buggiest place in all of Quetico. It was early July and mosquitoes were in top form. The moment the sun lowered itself below the treeline, the lowland swamp surrounding my site came alive with bugs. I escaped to my bug-shelter to cook a late dinner, using my one-burner stove, and didn't even bother to exit the shelter to set up my tent. I just rolled my Therm-a-rest over a patch of grass and snuggled inside my sleeping bag.

This wasn't my first time sleeping in the bug-shelter. In fact, I've come to choose it over the tent as long as bad weather is not in the forecast. I purchased

Everyone seems to laugh at my bug shelter — until the bugs start biting.

the item from Eureka a few years back and will never forget the first time packing it along on a trip. I was with some regular canoe buddies who always seem to tease me about my latest equipment purchase. They laughed hysterically at the bug-shelter; that is, until the bugs came out the first night and I refused to share my refuge. Since then, every member of the group has to give me a shot of their precious rum supply before being allowed in for the night.

The morning of day four was the most memorable for me. I awoke early, even brewed up my coffee while still wrapped up in my sleeping bag. And as I sipped on my morning java, peeking through the fine mesh of the shelter to watch the sun rise, a cow moose walked out on the opposite bank of the river. It was amazing. Famed canoeist and filmmaker Bill Mason was right when he stated in his film *Waterwalker*, "Nature films often give the impression that the country is running alive with animals. Well, I'll tell you right now, it's a lie. I'll canoe a whole summer and see one, two moose, maybe a bear if I'm lucky…It's a really big deal to see an animal."

After the moose sighting I spent a quiet morning paddling down a mild current to Kawa Bay, with only one undesignated portage and a liftover on a logjam. I finally felt calm. I had reached the next phase, made the transition of leaving the weight and stress of the real world behind and embraced my wild surroundings. I relaxed my pace a bit, even taking time to fish.

Kawa Bay is renowned for its walleye and pike angling. You just have to tow a line and lure behind you and you're bound to catch something. By the time I reached the central part of Kawnipi Lake, I had hooked and released over a dozen fish. Having had such good luck, I made the smart choice to call it an early day and fish some more. I made camp on one of the countless islands prior to Atkins Bay and dined that night on fried walleye fillets.

Again, many canoeists have chosen not to stay over on Kawa Bay or Kawnipi Lake since the 1995 fire passed through the area. But it's interesting to note that Kagaigon, Ojibwe chief of Kawa Bay, specifically chose land at the mouth of the Wawiag River to become their reserve in 1877, in the aftermath of another wildfire. He was mocked by R.B. Ross, surveyor of the reserve lands, for doing so. Ross claimed the land was "…a vast bed of stone, burnt land and fallen trees." When Ross returned a few years later, however, he realized how quickly the forest had bounced back and how right Kagaigon had been to select such a place to live.

The policies of forest fire suppression in Quetico have changed greatly throughout the park's history. Quetico's first rangers were expected to prevent wildfires at any cost. Logging companies looked upon fires as destruction of valuable timber. In 1917 the Forest Fire Prevention Act was created and fire lookout towers were established across the park, followed by the first aerial patrol by bushplane in 1921. In 1926 some local politicians felt that more roads were necessary to prevent forest fires in the park. Environmental groups not only opposed the road development but also began their long fight against fire suppression in the park. In 1997 the Ontario Ministry of Natural Resources announced that a

Moose sighting number three along the Wawiag River.

You just have to tow a line and lure behind you while crossing Kawnipi Lake, and you're bound to catch a mess of walleye.

Prescribed Natural Fire Zone was to be established in Quetico, stating that "to properly protect the natural heritage many natural ecosystems within Ontario's parks and conservation reserves require disturbance by fire for renewal."

Day five was spent paddling southeast down Kawnipi Lake's Atkins Bay, and then portaging around the Falls Chain. The series of eight cascades are considered to be among the most scenic places in Quetico, and among the most dangerous places to paddle (a number of canoeists have drowned here). The dangerous aspect is accurate if you're going downstream on the Maligne River, especially in high water. Most of the portages begin very close to the brink of falls, and the real danger occurs when tandem paddlers approach the takeout and the bow person gets out first. If that happens, the stern of the canoe has a good chance of swinging out into the current, sending it and the stern paddler over of the falls. I was traveling upstream, however, and the only major concern was to make sure I didn't drift sideways to the current, flip over, and get flushed into the churning water below the falls (tandem paddlers going upstream should make sure that they do the opposite and have the bow person get out first).

The first drop, Kennebas Falls, links Atkins Bay with Kenny Lake. Water levels were moderate, but there was a strong enough current below the falls to make me feel a little anxious, especially when I had to maneuver around a fallen tree just prior to the takeout. The put-in at the portage (10 rods/55 yd/50 m) is only a canoe length away from the brink of the falls, and I hugged the shoreline while pushing off into Kenny Lake.

Next was a 95-rod (520 yd/480 m) portage around Canyon Falls. It's also located on the right, directly across the mouth of a small inlet that heads to the portage leading to McEwen Lake. There are two takeouts, the foremost obviously used when high water and a fast current don't allow you to reach the second option. I was told about a shortcut up and over the island centering the falls, but I think this is only possible during extremely low water levels. Fortunately I was able to push myself up to the second takeout (the trail from the initial takeout is brutal). It wasn't easy. I had to grab onto some tree branches to help me from drifting out into the swift current. The extra section of trail, however, was steep, rocky and full of blow-downs. What remains is a tough scramble up a steep slope and around a few more blow-downs. This is definitely the worst portage along the entire Falls Chain.

The third carry is a 110-rod (605 yd/560 m) portage located on the right of an unnamed cascade and Koko Falls. The portage is rocky and has a few hills to contend with. It also has numerous side trails, most of which spur off to viewing areas for the two drops. One side trail allows canoeists to carry down and paddle the small pond between the two falls, reducing the portage by a few yards. The shortcut was definitely not worth getting in and out of the canoe, so I kept to the right all the way to the put-in.

Almost directly across from the last put-in is the next portage, a 16-rod (88 yd/80 m) trail to the left of Little Falls. The cascade is properly named since it's more of a chute than a falls. The portage itself was steep in some sections but relatively easy when compared to the previous carries. It was a little spooky, however, pushing away from the put-in. The current tugged at my canoe as I paddled hard up a small swift not far upstream from the big drop.

After a lunch stop at one of the campsites along Sidney Lake, which is actually just a widening of the Maligne River, I continued upstream, portaging again to the left. The trail (8 rods/44 yd/40 m) went over a slab of bare rock — perfectly matching the name of the cascade it avoided: Bald Rock Falls.

It was mid-afternoon by the time I completed the Bald Rock portage, and I was thankful that I had only two more short carries around Four Falls to finish for the day. I carefully ferried across to the right bank and found the first portage located in a small cove. It was uphill but also a quick and easy 20 rods (110 yd/100 m), and the only thing separating me from the next portage —55-rod (300 yd/280 m), also on the right — was a short paddle across a small lagoon. A side trail connects the two portages, making it unnecessary to paddle the short stretch of river between, and in retrospect I should have went for that option. It might even have been possible to line up the first chute and portage across the centre island. My chosen route was quite simple, however, and there wasn't any real need to find an easier way.

That night I camped out on some island on Saganagons Lake. It was late and it might have been a better choice to have stopped earlier, somewhere along the Falls Chain, but since Canyon Falls portage I had met up with numerous canoeists who were planning to camp on sites between the cascades.

I was glad to have found such a quiet place to camp on Saganagons because by the time I paddled over to the takeout at Dead Man's Portage the next morning, three large canoe groups had come up behind me. Thankfully the carry was quick and easy and I was able to get ahead of the crowds. The portage also acts as a great shortcut around Saganagons' Boundary Point. It's puzzling why it's given such an ominous title. The 58-rod (320 yd/290 m) trail is pretty straightforward, except for a rock ledge located about halfway en route.

After completing Dead Man's Portage another two groups of paddlers caught up with me while paddling down the southwest bay of Saganagos, towards the familiar Silver Falls portage, so I opted for the alternative route I had planned on taking at the beginning of the trip. The first portage, located just south of the large island in Saganagos southwest bay, measured 95 rods (522 yd/480 m). It wasn't a great distance to carry across, but halfway along I considered turning back and taking the Silver Falls portage instead. Deep muck, up to my knees in places, stood in the way, and I had to balance on rocks and logs strategically placed by previous users. After the first carry, there were only three short portages (all 10 rods/55 yd/50 m or less) linking a chain of lakes to Saganaga's Cache Bay.

To save some money I hadn't bothered to book a shuttle back across Saganaga Lake, so I was forced to spend a large part of my second-to-last day paddling this great expanse of water. The wind was up as well, and I didn't get that far beyond Cache Bay before deciding to call it a day. As it was my last night, I tried desperately to find a place to camp away from my fellow campers. I wasn't quite ready to be with people again. I had spent the majority of the trip alone, and I liked it that way. It had been the point of the trip in the first place. The solitude had helped calm my views on urban society, and I didn't want crowds of canoeists to undo the healing power of my time spent out here. I erected my tent on a small outcrop of rock in a secluded bay and began enjoying my privacy — that is, until a large group of Boy Scouts paddled into the bay adjacent to my island site and started setting up camp.

The noise seemed so intrusive. Scout leaders bellowed out commands, and the boys immediately became busy with their chores. The sound of clanging pots, canoes being hauled up on shore, wood being cut, it all seemed deafening. Their conversations echoed clearly across the lake. My frustration grew until it seemed my time in the wilderness had done nothing to alleviate my annoyance with society. I crawled into my tent that night angry and depressed. But as I fumbled about, trying desperately to look for something to stuff in my ears and drown out the noise, I heard the boys start up a rousing chorus of "Alice the Camel." The song ended in bouts of laughter, followed by another camp song classic, "Land of the Silver Birch." It was then, while listening to the kids' youthful enthusiasm, that I realized how foolish my mood was. These weren't the kids who had played havoc with my life back home. They weren't wandering the city streets loosening wheel bolts. These kids had direction in their lives, they were learning positive values, and there was no need for me to get angry. They were out in the wilderness, enjoying it just as I was.

Before they started up again I crawled out of my tent, walked to the darkened shoreline to applaud the singers, and then called out "Do you know 'Camp Fires Burning'?" There was more laughter, followed by a "hush" from one of the leaders, and then they sang:

> *Camp fires burning,*
> *Camp fires burning,*
> *Draw nearer,*
> *Draw nearer,*
> *In the glowing,*
> *In the glowing*
> *Come sing and be merry.*

I was ready to go home now, not only to deal with society's ills, but also to appreciate the good in humankind.

Wawiag River Loop

LENGTH: 6 days

PORTAGES: 18

LONGEST PORTAGE: 255 rods (1,400yd/1280 m)

DIFFICULTY: Intermediate canoe-tripping skills are required.

ACCESS: To reach the public launch on most southern inlet of Saganaga Lake, take the 56-mile (90 km) Cook County Lake Road (Gunflint Trail Road) to its very northwestern end. The road begins in the town of Grand Marais, Minnesota. The ranger station is located in Saganaga Lake's Cache Bay, on a small island not too far from the mouth of the bay. The majority of Saganaga Lake is American owned where motors not exceeding 25 horsepower are allowed. No motors are allowed on the Canadian side.

ALTERNATIVE ACCESS: None

TOPOGRAPHICAL MAPS: 52-B/2, 52-B/6, 52-B/7, 52-B/12

FISHER MAPS: F-19, F-25, F-26

The chain of remote, blue-tinted lakes west of Agnes Lake
holds some of the oldest white pine in North America.

9 The Pines Loop

IT'S INTERESTING HOW CANOEISTS are attracted to the familiar, a landscape they like to call their own. Algonquin is where I do most of my paddling, not only because it's near my home in Peterborough, Ontario, but also because it has what I like on a trip: deep, turquoise-colored lakes filled with trout and surrounded by large white pine. So it's no surprise that for one of my initial trips in Quetico I chose a route with much the same character. Located west of Agnes Lake is a circular trip made up of a series of seemingly bottomless, blue-tinted lakes that yield good-sized lake trout and have some of the oldest white pine in North America rooted along the shoreline.

The trip started at Prairie Portage, the most southern access point in Quetico, reached by paddling up Moose, Newfound and Sucker Lakes. I booked a boat shuttle with La Tourell's Moose Lake Outfitters, made it to the access point in 20 minutes, and then portaged 25 rods (138 yd/130 m) over to Basswood Lake. It was a quick way to get there. But then it took until noon to go through the line-up to register at the ranger cabin, leaving me only enough daylight to paddle across to Basswood's Burke Bay and carry over the trouble-free 90-rod (495 yd/450 m) portage into Burke Lake.

I had a quick breakfast of porridge and coffee the next morning so I could head out across Basswood Lake's North Bay before the winds picked up, and I was rewarded by spotting a black bear wading through the shallow parts of the creek connecting Burke Lake and North Bay. Two portages, measuring 10 rod (55 yd/50 m) and 14 rod (77 yd/70 m) are located at both ends of the creek and were quick and easy to carry across. There was even enough water in the weed-choked creek leading up the northeast corner of North Bay that I only had to get out and drag the canoe twice before reaching the 10-rod (55 yd/50 m) portage leading in to South Lake.

Another straightforward 10-rod (55 yd/50 m) carry, to the northeast and beside a small cascade tumbling into South Lake, took me into West Lake. And keeping to the right-hand shore of West Lake, I found two more portages leading in to Shade Lake. The first was approximately 20 rods (110 yd/100 m), going up a short incline and alongside another small waterfall, and the other was an uncomplicated 10-rod (55 yd/50 m) portage on the left-hand side of the creek.

Before continuing on, I drifted down the far northeastern bay of Shade Lake to check out the faded Native pictographs (two abstract thunderbirds) and then backtracked to carry over two additional portages: an 82-rod (450 yd/410 m) portage to an unnamed lake and, almost to the immediate right, a 123-rod (676 yd/620 m) portage to Grey Lake. The first carry wasn't a problem, but the longer one, into

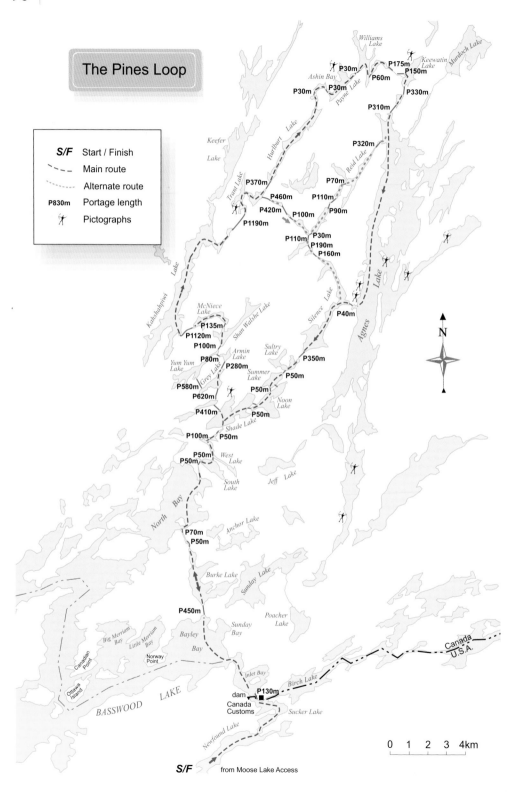

The Pines Loop

S/F — Start / Finish
- - - Main route
······ Alternate route
P830m Portage length
🏃 Pictographs

Williams Lake
P30m
P175m
Keewatin Lake
Murdoch Lake
Ashin Bay
P60m
P150m
P30m
P30m
Payne Lake
P330m
P30m
P310m
Keefer Lake
P320m
Reid Lake
P370m
P70m
P460m
P110m
P420m
P100m
P90m
Trant Lake
P1190m
P110m
P30m
P190m
P160m
Kahshahpiwi Lake
McNiece Lake
P135m
P1120m
Shan Walshe Lake
Silence Lake
P40m
Agnes Lake
P100m
P80m
Armin Lake
Sultry Lake
P580m
P280m
Summer Lake
P350m
Grey Lake
P620m
P50m
Yum Yum Lake
P50m
Noon Lake
P410m
P50m
Shade Lake
P100m
P50m
P50m
West Lake
P50m
South Lake
Jeff Lake
N
North Bay
Anchor Lake
P70m
P50m
Burke Lake
Sunday Lake
P450m
Poacher Lake
Big Merriam Bay
Little Merriam Bay
Bayley Bay
Sunday Bay
Norway Point
Canadian Point
Ottawa Island
Inlet Bay
Birch Lake
Canada U.S.A.
BASSWOOD LAKE
dam
Canada Customs
P130m
Sucker Lake
Newfound Lake
0 1 2 3 4km
S/F from Moose Lake Access

Grey, began and ended with a steep slope and a beaver meadow filled with boot-sucking mud. It's also a confusing trail to follow, with two takeouts and a very puzzling intersection just before the halfway point (when in doubt, go right).

Yum Yum Lake was next. It can be reached by either a 115-rod (632 yd/580 m) portage just to the left of the previous portage or two shorter portages in and out of Armin Lake, measuring 55 and 16 rods (302 yd/280 m and 88 yd/80 m). I took the easier route, of course, but it only took me to the far northeastern tip of Yum Yum and didn't allow me to check out the large pine growing along the lakeshore. Grey and Armin Lakes have their fair share of old-growth pine, and the next lake, connected to Yum Yum by a 20-rod (110 yd/100 m) portage, had some enormous trees. The lake was unnamed at the time of my trip but was named after park naturalist Shan Walshe the year he died (1991).

Shan had worked in Quetico since 1970 and wrote the essential flora guide for the park, *The Plants of Quetico and the Ontario Shield*. The Thunder Bay *Chronicle* called him "the *conscience* of Quetico." Shan Walshe was a humble man and an atypical parks employee who spent more time in the field than behind an administrative desk.

I met Shan during my first visit to the park. He was driving by and noticed me checking out some wildflowers. He immediately stopped to help identify them, and we spent a good hour together walking through the woods. In that brief time, he taught me more about forest ecology than I had learned in three years of academic study in forestry.

I considered staying on Shan Walshe Lake for my second night out, but I still had enough time and energy to do one more carry, a 27-rod (148 yd/135 m) portage linking the lower northwest corner of Shan Walshe to McNiece Lake. It was an easy walk, and the trail went straight through some of the most impressive old-growth pine of the entire trip. Some were over three feet in diameter and had to be at least 250 to 300 years of age. Campsites were limited on McNiece, however, and I ended up brushing out a spot on an outcrop of rock overlooking the western bay.

After dinner I paddled around the lake to check out the trees. White pine dominated, but there were also a few scattered old-growth red pine and cedar trees, some of which had to be close to 400 years old. The largest patch was along the northwest corner. I pulled the canoe ashore here and walked through the stand.

Red and white pine were never the main species in the park, and past logging practices made them even more scarce. The pine on McNiece Lake were scheduled to be cut in the 1960s until the government put a stop to the logging plan after receiving over 2,000 letters from concerned citizens. It was fire suppression, however, that did the most damage to this delicate environment. Wildfires open up areas of the forest and enrich the soil to allow for new growth. With thick bark and its main branches positioned higher up, an old-growth pine usually survives

Catching a lake trout is a quintessential part of canoe-tripping in Quetico.

a fire and helps regenerate the forest, but when the fires were suppressed in Quetico, spruce and balsam took over instead. While walking among the McNiece Lake stand, I noticed a few pine seedlings rooted below the larger trees, but I also noticed significant patches of young spruce and balsam taking hold. This ancient forest is changing, and not for the better.

The next day I carried southwest in to Kahshahpiwi Lake by way of a 223-rod (1,226 yd/1120 m) portage. This trail definitely gave me a workout. Near the end I descended into a swampy bog, then hauled myself out again by clambering up an almost sheer slab of rock. It was exhausting but not impossible; and besides, it was this rugged landscape that initially protected the pine from the logger's axe. To me, that's worth a bit of suffering.

I had a couple hours of paddling north on scenic Kahshahpiwi Lake before taking on another portage, this one leading to Trant Lake. It's a lengthy one as well, measuring 237 rods (1,305 yd/1190 m). But the trail wasn't as bad as the one coming out of McNiece. Getting there, however, was a little tough, since it was tucked away on the far end of Kahshahpiwi's northeast bay, and I had to pull the canoe up a shallow, muddy creek to reach the takeout along the right bank. The footing was difficult in some sections where ankle-twisting roots and rocks blocked the way, especially close to the put-in.

I spent a good hour at the bottom end of Trant Lake looking for the Native pictographs reported to be here. I finally spotted them near the base of a high cliff along the western shore, directly beside the bay where the portage comes into Trant Lake, a totally different location than suggested in my park booklet. The booklet also noted that a canoe with two paddlers and three moose could be discerned in the pictograph. But, to me, one of the moose resembled a snowshoe hare and another had straight antlers, which made it look more like a young elk.

From here I could head north through a chain of lakes leading to the top end of Agnes Lake or choose a shortcut west through a series of small unnamed lakes to Silence Lake, where I had planned on heading southwest back to the North Arm. I had traveled the shortcut before as a day trip from Agnes and remembered it to be a gorgeous area with clear blue lakes and magnificent white pine. It was also hardly used and the portages weren't all that difficult either. The first, measuring 90 rods (495 yd/460 m), was rocky at first, with a moderate hill midway (but with a nice view of the grassy creek below) and a muddy section near the end. The second (84 rods/462 yd/420 m) was about the same, except it pointed downhill most of the way. And the third (110 yd/100 m [20 rods] and marked to the left of a creek) was littered with boulders but had an incredible number of massive white pine growing near the put-in. What remained was quite easy, three somewhat rocky but short portages (22 rods/120 yd/110 m; 38 rods/210 yd/190 m; and 32 rods/176 yd/160 m), all marked to the left. The route was perfect, really, one of the best areas in the park in my opinion, but I had lots of time left in my trip and had no need for a shortcut, so I opted to head further north to Agnes before turning back.

I ended day three by carrying over one more portage, a very rocky but short uphill (74 rods/405 yd/370 m) from Trant to Hurlburt Lake. Even though Trant Lake had a number of spots to pitch a tent, Hurlburt had a few more options. It also had better fishing. That evening I dined on a two-pound smallmouth bass, smothered in butter and fresh lemon, then wrapped in tinfoil and baked in the hot coals of the campfire.

The rock cliffs along Payne Lake's Ahsin Bay hold some of the park's best pictographs.

Day four was the longest and the toughest of the trip. It didn't start off that badly. I managed to reach the top of Hurlburt Lake before 10:00 A.M. and made good time reaching Payne and William Lake. The map showed two portages linking an unnamed lake between Hurlburt and Payne. The first obstacle was just a liftover across a couple of logs midway up a shallow creek (there was a 6-rod/33 yd/30 m trail on the left); and the second was a quick 6-rod (33 yd/30 m) trail on the left; the second (same length) was a quick portage to the right of another rocky swift. The portage from Payne to William (on the right) wasn't even necessary; I was able to squeeze through the narrow channel connecting the two lakes. As a bonus, Payne Lake's Ahsin Bay held some incredible pictographs. The vibrant paintings — a thunderbird, cow moose, and an odd-looking fish — were located on the west side of the bay, just before the narrow inlet to the north. Surrounded by hills of pine and hemlock, William Lake was what I was searching for on my trip.

The difficult portion of my journey really didn't begin until I left William Lake by way of the 12-rod (66 yd/60 m) portage tucked away in the southeast corner. It began to rain during my carry-over, and then poured rain as I made my way over the 35-rod (192 yd/175 m) portage down to Hurlburt Creek. The trail hadn't been used for quite some time and thick brush closed in from all directions. But at least I found this portage. The next wasn't so easy. My map indicated that the trail was just to the left of where Hurlburt Creek flushes into the Keewatin Lake. It's not! During a trip a few years later, I discovered that the portage actu-

The route between Trant and Keewatin Lake can be difficult at times, but it is also incredibly scenic and rewarding.

ally exits the creek well before this and climbs down 30 rods (165 yd/150 m) toward a small bay, north of where the creek comes in. On this trip, however, I never found it. Instead I spent a good hour dragging my gear and canoe straight through a large patch of spruce trees rooted along the left side of the waterway. My actions were quite comical: there I was, trying to keep my feet dry by jumping from one boulder to the other, while at the same time the rain was drenching me from head to foot.

Keewatin Lake features a group of pictographs not far up from the creek, along the west shoreline. It consists of scattered individual paintings (an overweight moose, a thunderbird, a faded zigzag line) and a main cluster (canoe with two paddlers, two thunderbirds, and what seems to be a moose and cross). The zigzag line is probably the most interesting, since it's supposed to be a record of the artist's lifeline, one that changed direction many times.

Keewatin is Ojibwe for "northwest wind," a word that didn't match the character of the lake when I was on it. The wind was directly from the south, a big problem since I was planning on paddling over half the length of Agnes Lake before calling it a day. I tried to convince myself the wind wouldn't be that big an issue once I reached Agnes Lake. But after carrying in and out of an unnamed lake prior to Agnes, connected by an uphill 65-rod (358 yd/330 m) portage with a few ankle-twisting rocks and a 62-rod (358 yd/310 m) portage with a slightly sloped takeout, I quickly realized my anxiety was well justified. The wind was whipping up the water something fierce, and I found it difficult enough to push off from the put-in, let along paddle down the lake. I started my way across Agnes at 2:30 P.M. and found myself lifting over the 8-rod (44 yd/40 m) trail of rock and mud leading to Silence Lake just after 8:00 P.M.

In hindsight I should have seriously considered taking a side route off the top end of Agnes and down Reid Lake and a series of unnamed lakes to Silence. But I knew nothing about the difficulty of the portages en route (eight in total, the shortest being 6 rods/33 yd/30 m and the longest being 64 rods/352 yd/320 m), and I just couldn't pass up the chance to explore Agnes Lake. The lake has always been a popular destination for canoeists because of its natural beauty, but more importantly, it was a gathering place for Native people as well, and six known pictograph sites are found here, and one very unique petroglyph.

Due to the heavy winds blowing across Agnes, I had to keep to the western shoreline and could only check out two of the Native sites. Too bad, the southern end of the lake has two newly discovered sites, a "Maymaygwayshi" (mischievous spirit people living among the cracks in the cliff and who act as a go-between with the spirit world) and two figures in a canoe. The elongated bay to the east has a faded "X" on a tan rock and a moose or caribou, and the westernmost of two central islands holds the largest collection, whose images consist of a small bear, a cross, another canoe with two occupants, and a number of hand smears and other indistinguishable red wash marks.

The sites I did check out were noteworthy. Both were located just north of the portage in to Silence Lake. The first pictograph was of two snowshoe hares. These symbols are rare in the park but are extremely important in the spiritual culture of the Ojibwe. The hare was one of the few species that didn't abandon Spirit Woman, who gave birth to all animals during the creation of the earth. The hare was also the animal that was always plentiful when others were not, and thus saved the people from starvation.

`Only about 10 rods (55 yd/50 m) south of the pictograph site is the Native petroglyphs. They are images chiseled into the rock rather than painted on them, and they are the only known petroglyphs in the Quetico and Boundary Waters region. They depict four caribou, indicating a herd, which has led some experts to speculate that barrenland caribou once existed here before the solitary woodland caribou. If this is true, it would make the petroglyphs hundreds of years older than any known Native paintings.

My stay on Silence Lake was fitting. I camped just south of the portage, along the eastern shoreline, and had the lake to myself. It was one of the most peaceful sleeps I've ever had. Sigurd Olson said this in one of his essays in *Songs of the North*: "This [silence] was more than temporary release from noise, it was a primordial thing that seeped into the deepest recesses of the mind until mechanical intrusions were intolerable."

From Silence Lake my route headed southwest, back to familiar Shade Lake. The first portage was the longest of the day, measuring 70 rods (385 yd/350 m). It was a bit confusing to follow; going right of a creek, over bare rock, through a strip of meadow grass, over the creek, then forking off in all directions toward the put-in at Sultry Lake. It was one of those trails where you weren't exactly lost, just confused as to your exact whereabouts most of the time.

Then a 10-rod (55 yd/50 m) trail located in the far left corner of Sultry Lake took me up a moderate slope and in to Summer Lake. From here it was a choice of two portages to Noon Lake. Both were located along the left shoreline and both were approximately 10 rods (55 yd/50 m) in length. The only difference was that the first one was up a steeper hill than the second, but not so much steeper that I elected not to use it. A choice of two 10-rod (55 yd/50 m) trails also existed from the northwest corner of Noon Lake to Shade Lake. And again, there wasn't much difference between the two. So, to be different, I chose the second rather than the first this time.

From Shade Lake I backtracked to Basswood Lake's North Bay through West and South Lake, spending my last night on an island on the northeast corner. It was an early finish, especially when compared to the previous 12-hour day, and I only had to head back to Prairie Portage by way of Burke Lake and Bayley Bay on my final day out. Besides, the campsite I chose had a tent spot situated under an old pine and overlooking the tranquil blue waters of the bay. I had found the familiar in a place that I wasn't familiar with in the beginning. And it was a route, I later discovered, that would become my favorite in all of Quetico.

The Pines Loop

LENGTH: 5–7 days

PORTAGES: 38

LONGEST PORTAGE: 1,305 yd/1190 m (237 rods)

DIFFICULTY: Advanced novice to intermediate canoe-tripping skills are required.

ACCESS: Prairie Portage Ranger Station is reached by paddling north on Moose, Newfound and Sucker Lakes, and then portaging 28 rods (154 yd/140 m) over to Basswood Lake. The cabin is to your right. But before that, you must drive northeast out of Ely, Minnesota. Take Highway 169 (Fernberg Road) and then Moose Lake Road. It's 19 miles (31 km) from Ely to the public launch.

ALTERNATIVE ACCESS: None

TOPOGRAPHICAL MAPS: 52-B/3, 52-B/4, 52-B/5, 52-B/6

FISHER MAPS: F-10, F-18, F-25

Alana was a little less interested in retracing Leopold's route than I was.
She just used it as an excuse to go paddling.

10 Leopold's North Country Loop

I'LL ADMIT THAT IT MAY HAVE SEEMED A LITTLE ODD: two Canadian canoeists wanting to enter to the United States so that they can re-enter Canada's Quetico Park from the U.S. side and thereby retrace the historic route taken by American conservationist Aldo Leopold. The U.S. border guard found the whole idea a bit too quirky, but I wasn't about to let one man in uniform deter us from our quest, so I broke all border-crossing etiquette, and rather than politely agreeing with him and retreating back to Canada, I launched into a long spiel about how important the trip was to us. My speech was short. I only got to the part about my long-time desire to visit the same lakes and rivers that Aldo Leopold, a wilderness visionary and author of the quintessential environmental book *Sand County Almanac*, when the guard simply waved us through. I'm not sure if he suddenly agreed with the reasoning behind our trip or just couldn't bear to listen to my long-winded explanation, but he let us pass. In a couple of hours my wife Alana and I, along with our dog Bailey, arrived at Ely, Minnesota, to begin our pilgrimage.

We accessed Quetico Provincial Park just as Leopold did in 1924, by way of the remote ranger station situated on Basswood Lake's Prairie Portage. There were a few differences, however. Leopold had paddled across Fall Lake in the Boundary Waters before reaching Basswood Lake; we went across Moose Lake, Newfound Lake and Sucker Lake. Alana and I also made use of an outfitter's boat shuttle service, reducing the rather dull two-hour paddle to Prairie Portage to a mere 20 minutes. Once we arrived, and portaged the 25 rods (138 yd/130 m) across to Canada, we still had to wait in line for over an hour before being able to register. It was raining, and Alana and I had to share the line-up with some curi-ous characters, including those decked out in full military fatigues, with machetes and canteens full of cheap Scotch. Bailey, our hyperactive Springer Spaniel, was the only one who didn't mind waiting, as the militaristic bunch ahead of us had a male Golden Retriever that she fancied.

Eventually we were on our way, paddling full tilt down the middle of Basswood Lake, with

It's the oddest thing to paddle down Basswood Lake, with Canada on one side and the United States on the other.

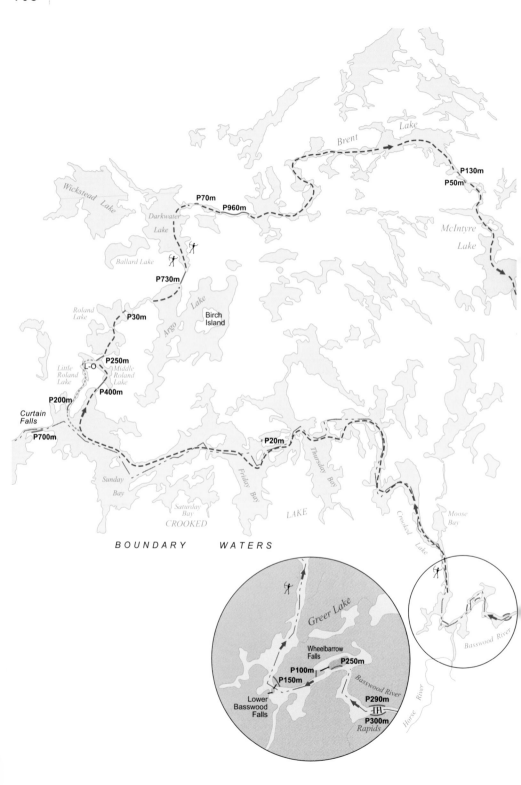

Wickstead Lake

Darkwater Lake

P70m

P960m

Brent Lake

P130m

P50m

McIntyre Lake

Ballard Lake

P730m

Roland Lake

Argo Lake

P30m

Birch Island

P250m

L-O

Little Roland Lake

Middle Roland Lake

P400m

P200m

Curtain Falls

P700m

P20m

Friday Bay

Thursday Bay

Sunday Bay

Saturday Bay

CROOKED   **LAKE**

Crooked Lake

Moose Bay

BOUNDARY   WATERS

Basswood River

Greer Lake

Wheelbarrow Falls

P100m

P250m

P150m

Lower Basswood Falls

Basswood River

P290m

P300m

Rapids

Horse River

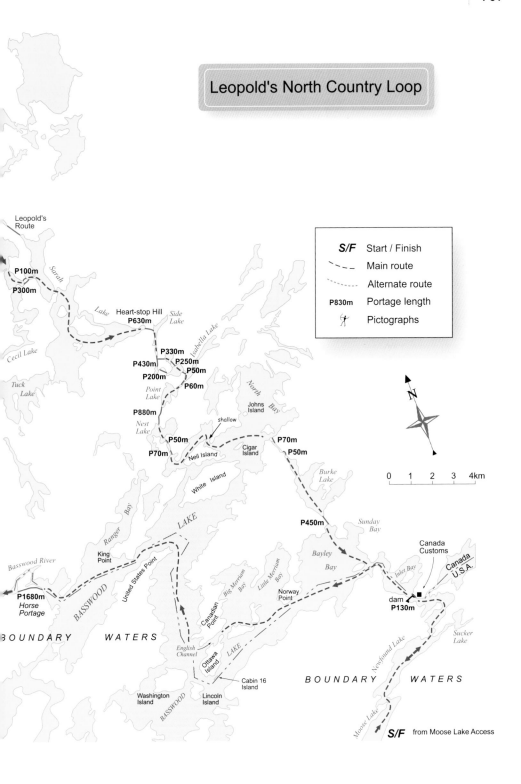

Leopold's North Country Loop

Legend:

S/F	Start / Finish
– – –	Main route
·····	Alternate route
P830m	Portage length
🏹	Pictographs

Leopold's Route

P100m
P300m

Sarah Lake

Heart-stop Hill
P630m

Side Lake

Cecil Lake

Tuck Lake

Isabella Lake

P330m
P430m
P250m
P50m
P200m
P60m

Point Lake

P880m

Nest Lake

North Bay

Johns Island

shallow

P50m
P70m

Neil Island

Cigar Island

P70m
P50m

White Island

Burke Lake

P450m

Sunday Bay

Ranger Bay

King Point

United States Point

BASSWOOD LAKE

Bayley Bay

Canada Customs

Canada U.S.A.

Basswood River

P1680m
Horse Portage

Big Merriam Bay

Little Merriam Bay

Norway Point

Inlet Bay

dam
P130m

Sucker Lake

BOUNDARY   WATERS

Canadian Point

English Channel

Ottawa Island

LAKE

Cabin 16 Island

BOUNDARY   WATERS

Newfound Lake

Washington Island

Lincoln Island

BASSWOOD

Moose Lake

S/F from Moose Lake Access

N

0 1 2 3 4km

Laundry day on Basswood Lake.

the United States to the left of us and Canada to the right. To mark the occasion, we fastened an American flag to one gunwale and a Canadian flag to the other.

Alana and I made it all the way down Basswood Lake and set up camp at 4:00 P.M. We had traveled a good distance. Much further than Leopold's group (Leopold, his brothers Carl and Frederic, and son Starker) on their first day. They had only paddled a mile out from Prairie Portage. Our greater progress had a lot to do with the fact that the Leopold party set aside time each day to troll for pike, pickerel and lake trout, which easily made this average seven-day trip into a full fifteen-day excursion.

Both groups, ours and theirs, chose to camp on the Canadian side of Basswood. Leopold's gang preferred it simply because it was more scenic, stating that "the pine timber on the Canadian side is all uncut and not much burned, while on the American side there is not a pine left."

The pine forest still seemed healthier on the Canadian side when Alana and I passed through. But our decision to camp there was based solely on the fact that we had not purchased a permit for the Boundary Waters, leaving us only able to camp on Quetico sites.

Local outfitters suggested that we acquire permission to camp in either park, but we honestly couldn't be bothered after taking so much time to arrange everything else for our trip. First, we had to purchase a Remote Area Border Crossing Permit through Canadian Customs. We then had to barter with dozens of outfitters working out of Ely to book our boat shuttle and vehicle storage (La Tourell's

Resort won out in the end). Two separate fishing licenses had to be bought, neither of which we ever made use of. Paperwork for our dog, Bailey, had to be prepared. And then we had to deal with the daunting task of getting a reservation for one of the busiest access points in Quetico. Entry points don't restrict where you go or how long you go for, but admission is based on a quota system, and Prairie Portage allows only two groups per day to pass through, which forced us to reserve at least five months in advance.

What saved us in the end was Quetico's "wilderness concept" philosophy. To enhance the canoeist's experience, campsites are not marked in the interior. With that in mind, you can camp anywhere within the boundaries of the park as long as you practice low-impact camping. And even though most lakes have obvious campsites due to years of continuous use, we never had to worry about finding a place to erect our tent.

By 9:00 A.M. the next morning, Alana, Bailey and I found ourselves carrying around Horse Portage, to your left, the first of four portages on the Basswood River. The waterway connects Basswood Lake with Crooked Lake via a series of falls and turbulent rapids. It's rated as one of the most captivating places in all of Quetico. Horse Portage is also an easy carry, which is great, since it's 334 rods (1,837 yd/1680 m) long. The only problem was the crowds. By the time we reached the end, we had seen a grand total of 112 canoeists and kayakers. I'm not kidding! The side effects of having so many people utilize one area was also quite obvious: garbage littered the trails, mounds of toilet paper were found only a short distance away, and the stench of fish guts polluted the takeout.

The second portage, not far downstream, is also an easy carry. It has two portages, one on the American side and the other on the Canadian shore. Both measure approximately 60 rods (330 yd/300 m), and the only difference is that the American trail has a better put-in.

The river twists to the right, and it's another ten minutes of paddling before you have to get out and portage again, this time around Wheelbarrow Falls. You have two options here. You can take a 50-rod (275 yd/250 m) trail to the right of the main cascade or paddle around a channel to the far right and then take a shorter 20-rod (110 yd/100 m) portage to the right of a side chute. Alana and I took the smaller trail, but I was told later by other canoeists that the first option is the preferred choice. Either way, it's an easy carry.

Only one more portage remained for us before we could paddle out into the expanse of Crooked Lake and finally escape the crowds. It measured only 30 rods (165 yd/150 m) and had a huge takeout well back from the brink of Lower Basswood Falls. The only problem was that a cluster of 26 canoes and kayaks, which had caught up to us from the busy portage upstream, blocked the way. Alana and I had to wait a good 20 minutes before we could unload. To make matters worse, half the boats were owned by a girls' youth camp that had stopped to

According to Leopold, an international boundary marker makes a good tent peg.

swim above the falls but couldn't be bothered making room for other canoeists passing through. (We later learned that not long after we left, two of the girls and a leader had tumbled over the falls, and that the leader had died.)

The Lower Basswood Falls experience was a little different for Leopold's' party. Having camped near the takeout to the portage, they met only a solitary Native, who "chanced along in a birch-bark canoe." And the only sign of civilization was an International Boundary monument, which they used for a tent peg.

He did show concerns, however, over the busyness of Basswood Lake, labeling it the "civilized" portion of their route. Leopold knew even then that it was quite possible for mobs of tourists, especially those who prefer "mechanized recreation," to threaten wilderness travel. "To cherish we must see and fondle," he wrote in a discouraging form, "and when enough have seen and fondled, there is no wilderness left."

It was for this reason that Leopold's group, upon reaching Curtain Falls at the far western end of Crooked Lake, made the decision to "strike off north into wilder country." Alana and I gladly followed suit. After making camp close to Curtain Falls our third night, we portaged north into Roland Lake using a grown-over 80-rod (440yd/400 m) bush trail to Middle Roland and a 50-rod (275 yd/250 m) portage that begins a short way up a creek coming out of Roland, on the left-hand side. The regular route is up the Siobhan River (Little Roland Lake), using an easy 40-rod (220 yd/200 m) portage to the left of where the river flows into Crooked Lake, a short liftover to the left of where a small cascade flushes out of Middle Roland, and then the 50-rod (275 yd/250 m) portage into Roland. The bush trail was obviously more difficult, but it was also the way Alana and I believed Leopold's group had gone.

From Roland to Sarah Lake, a distance that took us four leisurely days, we saw no other canoeists. It was absolute bliss. Leopold also found solace here. His first evening, camping on Roland Lake, he wrote in his journal: "The number of adventures awaiting us in the blessed country seems without end. Watching the gray twilight settling upon our lake we could truly say that 'all our ways are pleasantness and all our paths are peace.'"

This was obviously a magical place for Leopold. It was also a pivotal time in his life. By that time he had written several articles, most dealing with wilderness values and all containing ideas highly accepted by his peers. He had just been given the job as associate director of the Forest Products Laboratory in Madison, Wisconsin. Just two weeks prior to his canoe trip, Leopold had been informed that his work on helping to preserve the first piece of official wilderness in a National Forest, the headwaters of New Mexico's Gila River, had been a success. He even confessed some years later that the Quetico trip might have been the best that he and his brothers ever made.

Surprisingly, the landscape has changed little since Leopold's time. Alana and I had similar wildlife sightings: moose, deer, beaver, bald eagles, grouse, loons, and an assortment of other waterfowl. And the lakes themselves still had "the green water of the real north country, rather than the brown water of Crooked and Basswood Lakes."

There were a few differences, the most notable being regeneration of the stands of fire-destroyed pine that Leopold's group had witnessed on the 145-rod (798 yd/730 m) portage between Argo and Darky Lake (recently reassigned its original name, Darkwater Lake). Another variance between the two trips was that Alana and I found the Native paintings Leopold had failed to locate on Darkwater Lake. It's a shame Leopold never saw the pictographs. They were the highlight of our trip. We had already seen paintings on Crooked Lake, located about a mile below Lower Basswood Falls, just to the north of an imposing overhang, but the Crooked Lake site is quite extraordinary and includes a pelican with horns and a moose smoking a pipe. We found the Darkwater Lake paintings to be the best we've ever witnessed. The first site, on the west shore of the south bay, depicts "Maymaygwayshi" (mischievous, hairy-faced little men who dwell in the cracks of the cliff). The second site, on the east shore of the south bay, depicts two small moose (one of which is missing its heart), a man firing a projectile, and a horned serpent known as Misshepezhieu overturning a group of canoes.

Witnessing this spiritual place was nothing short of spectacular. I immediately unpacked my camera, even though prior to our trip an Ojibwe elder had warned me not to photograph the images. He told me it would anger the spirits, especially those of the Maymaygwayshi and Misshepezhieu. But I didn't listen. Halfway through the roll of film, my camera lens broke. I replaced it, only to have my light meter suddenly stop working after clicking two more frames. I got the message.

We made generous offering of tobacco and got the heck out of there, but in less than 20 minutes a storm blew across the lake, and Alana and I found ourselves windbound not far from the paintings. The storm raged on through the night, and when we awoke the next morning we discovered our tent was crawling with wood ticks. Performing a "tick check," we found one on Alana's neck, two under my armpit, and five embedded in poor Bailey's ears.

Maybe all these mishaps were mere coincidences. It was definitely odd, however, that once we portaged out of Darkwater Lake our luck started to change for the better. The weather was absolutely stunning, and the wind was at our backs the entire day.

We paddled the Darkwater River connecting us to Brent Lake. Twenty minutes into it, we performed a quick carry over a 14-rod (77 yd/70 m) portage along the left bank, and then soon after, a much lengthier 190-rod (1,045 yd/960 m) portage, also to the left. The longer portage worked its way around a series of ponds, the last that you have to actually paddle across to finish the remaining 10 rods (55 yd/50 m) of trail.

The remainder of our day was spent paddling across the expanse of Brent and McIntyre Lakes. Brent Lake, made up of a series of narrow, twisting channels, is more like a river than a lake at times. It was tough to catch enough wind here to sail the canoe. It blew steadily out of the northwest, but because the lake zigzagged all over the place, we couldn't seem to keep the tarp up long enough to snag a breeze.

It was late afternoon by the time we reached the other side of Brent. Alana and I should have stopped here, but it was such a pleasant day, and the only thing between us and McIntyre were two short but rugged portages, one 25 rods/138 yd/130 m and the other 10 rods/55 yd/50 m, linking an unnamed lake between the southeast bay of Brent and the far northern end of McIntyre. We went for it, and ended the day with a late peanut-butter-and-jelly-sandwich dinner on a gorgeous island campsite.

Our extra time on the water on day four allowed us a much more leisurely pace on day five. We spent a good deal of the morning doing laundry (something Alana insists on doing halfway through any trip) and then explored a narrow inlet in the northwest corner of McIntyre Lake. Apparently Leopold took a portage here to connect with Sarah Lake. Our map showed no evidence of a trail and none existed. We did manage to walk through the thick brush to Sarah, but decided it would be foolish to carry our canoe and gear through. Our dog, Bailey, even refused to shoulder her pack. Alana and I managed to spook a moose before returning to the canoe and paddling south of McIntyre to take the present-day portage.

There's a choice of two trails. I only knew of the 20-rod (110 yd/100 m) portage, known as "the hill." It's an incredibly steep downhill ramble through ankle-breaking boulders to a poor put-in spot. The other portage, a rarely used

60-rod (330 yd/300 m) trail, is just to the south. It's obviously longer, but is supposed to be much easier.

We camped on Sarah Lake for two full days. The extended stay wasn't scheduled, and it meant we would have to push hard over the next couple of days to end the trip on time, but our campsite was just too perfect to leave. It was situated in the remote northeast corner of the lake, with a steep mound of rock to sit on and watch the sun set and a ridiculous amount of blueberries to munch on for breakfast. Besides, Alana and I suspected that it wouldn't be long after leaving Sarah Lake that we would start seeing the crowds again. We

Dog-tired on Sarah Lake.

were right. The moment we reached the portage leading out of Sarah Lake's southeast corner, we encountered a dozen paddlers lining up to use the trail.

You have two choices for getting from Sarah to Side Lake, either a steep 125-rod (688 yd/630 m) portage labeled "Heart-stop Hill" or a creek with three separate trails. And once again, I only knew about the steep one. The creek has some elevation on the first and second carry (27 rods/48 yd/135 m and 22 rods/120 yd/110 m, respectively), and there's mud to contend with on the remaining 7 rods (38 yd/35 m), but it's no "heart-stopper." Just make sure to paddle to the right when creek splits after the first carry.

We also had more than one option heading out of Side Lake. The initial portage, located at the southern corner of the lake, splits close to the takeout. Here, an alternative route goes right, in and out of an unnamed pond. But Alana and I kept to the regular route, a 65-rod (358 yd/330 m) goat trail with a much steeper grade than the previous portage. We weren't sure if going right would have been easier, but everyone we saw heading in and out of Side Lake seemed to be using the trail to the left.

Thankfully, things got easier after we carried out of Side Lake. From there we paddled across another unnamed lake, up a shallow creek clogged with dead-heads, and then began a 50-rod portage (275 yd/250 m) to the left of an old beaver dam. We sprinted across two relatively flat portages, the first being a 10-rod (55 yd/50 m) trail to the right of a creek entering the lower end of Isabella Lake, and the second a 12-rod (66 yd/60 m) trail going from the south end of Isabella to Point Lake.

Alana and I were surprised to see how unused the portage to Point Lake was. I guess most paddlers (except for Aldo Leopold) head up to the top end of Isabella to connect with Basswood Lake's North Bay. But Point Lake is extremely scenic, with turquoise waters and three incredible campsites. We stopped at the first site and rested from the previous uphill slog, and even caught a few decent-size bass.

With Point Lake's seeming lack of use, we worried about the 175-rod (962 yd/880 m) portage that would take us out to Nest Lake, but again it was surprisingly easy, only a bit of mud to be dealt with. Fifteen minutes later we were paddling across Nest Lake and taking on two rocky but short 10-rod and 14-rod (55 yd/50 and 77 yd/70 m) portages in and out of a shallow, mucky pond. That's when we realized why people don't generally travel this way. If the water level had been any lower, I doubt we could have got through.

Water level also became an issue while we traveled along the north channel of North Bay's Neil Island. It was a quicker route than having to paddle all the way around the south side, but a number of large boulders and blown-down pine trees kept us guessing as to the best route through.

The downed pines were remnants of the giant windstorm that hit the park back in 1999. It swept through the Boundary Waters and Quetico Provincial Park on July 4, downing 12 million trees and endangering hundreds of canoeists. Surprisingly, there were no deaths. But many were injured, and search-and-rescue teams worked for days to extract people from the interior. Countless stories have been told by the survivors, all of whom have called it one of the worst sudden storms they've ever witnessed. Former Park Ranger Art Madsen, who was paddling with his daughter on Saganaga Lake when the squall hit, recorded one of the best descriptions, in the Quetico Foundation's quarterly newsletter: "I could see it was coming fast and black clouds had a brown yellowish color under them. Lightning and thunder were flashing all around and wind was really getting up. After a few miles I was following along a rock wall, as I know lightning will hit the highest part. Quick as a flash I did not see the lightning but one of the loudest thunder cracks I'd ever heard nearly knocked my ears off. Then I could see this grayish wall of cloud coming fast and knew it would really put down heavy rain. When I crossed by Powells' place the wind was so strong it was pushing rain hor-

Surprisingly, Alana and I found little had changed since Leopold's trip in Quetico.

izontally. I was coming into the dock area very fast. My granddaughter rushed out and snubbed my bow rope to the dock. Within minutes the waves became 5 feet. This was the worst storm in memory." (Art was 94 at the time.)

Relieved to be out in open water, Alana and I decided to sail across, first to Cigar Island and then to where our map showed a portage heading in to Burke Lake. And, once again, we had two options. We took the first one we came to, just after a small island campsite and before the elongated point along the south shore. The portage was less than 10 rods (55 yd/50 m), but we had to wade up a small gravel swift before completing it. The put-in and takeout were full of huge rocks that marked up our canoe and frustrated the hell out of poor Bailey (her legs are much shorter than ours). Only after we completed our trip across did we become aware of the second route that began a little further past the point. It measured 14 rods (77 yd/70 m) but was a much easier trail.

To end our day, a very long one at that, Alana and I took on one more obstacle before making camp. We waded up a shallow creek, luckily with sand at the bottom and not boot-sucking muck, and then portaged over an easy 10-rod (55 yd/50 m) trail to Burke Lake.

All that remained for us the last two days out was a well-worn 90-rod (495 yd/450 m) portage from Burke to Basswood Lake's Bayley Bay and the familiar Prairie Portage.

Seeing the crowds pick up again once we arrived on Basswood Lake was deflating in a way. We were now seasoned trippers. We no longer craved soda pop or fast-food. We had gone from pulling on our rain jackets the moment the first drop was felt to not even bothering to put a rain jacket on at all until it started to pour. We watched in disbelief as the hordes of canoes and kayaks made their way into the park. By the time we approached the familiar Prairie Portage, we had encountered 148 more.

Solitude quickly became a thing of the past. Alana and I even had to race a gang of kayakers down the lake to get a campsite for our last night out. The site was less than perfect, situated directly across from the Canadian ranger station. Garbage littered the spot and noisy motorboats buzzed by constantly. Light rain began to fall just after dinner, and we ended our day early by heading in the tent to catch up on our reading. Alana had packed along a paperback novel, and I, of course, had brought Leopold's classic *Sand County Almanac*.

It was the content of this book that later caused environmentalists to call Leopold the "father of the new conservation movement." Sadly, Leopold died the same year his book went to print (1949), and he would never know how inspirational his writing would become to so many people. According to historian, Donald Fleming, Leopold was "the Moses of the New Conservation impulse of the 1960s and 1970s, who handed down the Tablets of the Law but did not live to enter the promised land."

Of all the short essays in *Sand County Almanac*, my favorite has to be "Thinking Like a Mountain," in which Leopold tells the tale of shooting a mother wolf:

> *We reached the old wolf in time to watch a fierce green fire dying in her eyes. I realized then, and have known ever since, that there was something new to me in those eyes — something known only to her and the mountain. I was young then, and full of trigger-itch. I thought that because fewer wolves meant more deer, then no wolves would mean hunters' paradise. But after seeing the green fire die, I sensed that neither the wolf nor the mountain agreed with such a view.*

Reading the wolf story that evening on Basswood Lake got me thinking. Leopold used the wolf as a way to measure the health of a wild place. The spirit of the wolf, of wilderness, was seen dying in its eyes that day on the mountain. The question is, has the "fierce green fire" now faded in Leopold's beloved north country? After all, he had seen no one in ten days; Alana and I had seen no one in just four. As I closed the book and switched off my headlamp, the answer came to me in the form of a single wolf howl. Yes, the fire was still very much alive.

Leopold's North Country Loop

LENGTH: 7–8 days

PORTAGES: 27

LONGEST PORTAGE:
334 rods (1,837 yd/1680 m)

DIFFICULTY: Advanced novice to intermediate canoe-tripping skills are required.

ACCESS: Prairie Portage Ranger Station is reached by paddling north on Moose, Newfound and Sucker Lakes, and then portaging 28 rods (154 yd/140 m) over to Basswood Lake. The cabin is to your right. But before that, you must drive northeast out of Ely, Minnesota. Take Highway 169 (Fernberg Road) and then Moose Lake Road. It's 19 miles (31 km) from Ely to the public launch.

ALTERNATIVE ACCESS: None

TOPOGRAPHICAL MAPS:
52-B/3, 52-B/4, 52-B/5

FISHER MAPS: F-9, F-10, F-17, F-18

11 Hunter Island Loop

ACCORDING TO PARK REGULARS, the ultimate Quetico canoe trip is the Hunter Island loop. Glancing at the map, however, it's hard to grasp why: for the most part, the route is made up of large, windy lakes; it passes through some of the busiest access points; the trip itself measures over 200 miles (320 km) and takes at least 12 days to complete; and it's not even a real island, just a land mass that splits the two historically significant fur-trade waterway routes, Kaministquia and Grand Portage. The only real reason I gave it a try was that one of my frequent canoemates, Andy Baxter, is one of those "park regulars," and he had repeatedly praised Hunter Island as a definitive Quetico canoe trip and wouldn't allow me to ignore it as a route for this guidebook.

So we chose a couple of weeks in June to paddle the loop, and after completing the route I had to admit that Andy was right, the Hunter Island trip is an essential Quetico canoe trip. Mind you, our trip did have a few shortcomings: an early June timeline made for one of the buggiest trips of my life; wind was a huge issue on some of the larger lakes; we met up with vast crowds of canoeists along the border lakes; and even at the end of the trip, I still couldn't grasp the "island" idea. What I did find, however, was that we paddled and portaged past so many natural and historical treasures, which typify what Quetico is really all about.

We started at the French Lake access. This is definitely not the norm, as it adds two or three extra days of paddling to the trip. Most paddlers link up with the central loop from the west, south or southeast end of the park, but that's due to the fact that over 80 percent of the paddlers in Quetico are from the United States. Andy and I chose French Lake for two main reasons. We were both Canadians, so logistically it was much easier to begin at a common access point in Canada. The second reason was that the northern portion of the park is less busy, and there's nothing worse than beginning Quetico's "ultimate canoe route" battling through crowds of other canoeists.

Our plan worked perfectly. In the two days of paddling French Lake–Pickerel Lake–Dore Lake–Twin Lakes–Sturgeon Lake (see Sturgeon Lake–Olifaunt Lake Loop for route description), we encountered only four other groups. The previous season I had started a trip from Ely's Moose Lake and counted 226 canoes in the first hour and a half of the trip. Andy and I had definitely made the right decision.

Day three was spent paddling almost the entire length of Sturgeon Lake. The wind direction was against us, but it only amounted to a slight breeze most of the time, pleasant enough to keep the blackflies and mosquitoes down a bit while we crept along the northern shore.

Camp was made just prior to the large bay where Jean Creek empties into the lake. It was a gorgeous spot, so much so that we questioned the reasoning behind a Quetico annual tradition called the Hunter Island Canoe Race, in which canoeists from all over attempt to break the speed record for paddling around Hunter Island. The times are impressive, with the latest record set in 1994 when Dan Litchfield and Steve Park, both from Ely, made it around the island in 28 hours, 49 minutes and 7 seconds. To do this, the racers spend a large part of the trip paddling in complete darkness. Even during daylight hours they are so focused on speed that they probably don't notice much of their natural surroundings. It's as if they're trying to battle nature rather than become part of it. Andy and I had more of the latter in mind.

Rarely am I up and out of the tent before Andy, but what awaited us on day four had me outside brewing morning coffee a half-hour before sunrise. The plan that day was to paddle down the Maligne River to Tanner Lake, then camp near Tanner Rapids. The Maligne River is one of the most scenic portions of the route, but it was Tanner Rapids that heightened my anticipation, the opportunity to visit the very spot where John Tanner was shot and left for dead, creating one of the most unique stories of the north ever published.

John Tanner was kidnapped by a group of Shawnee at the age of nine, then later sold to an Ojibwe woman near Lac la Croix for a keg of rum. For the next 30 years, Tanner lived as a Native, married a Native woman, and raised a family in a Native community. Later in his life, however, he made the decision to integrate his children into white society. It was this decision that nearly cost him his life at Tanner Rapids.

John Tanner was shot here in 1823,
creating one of the most unique stories of the North ever published.

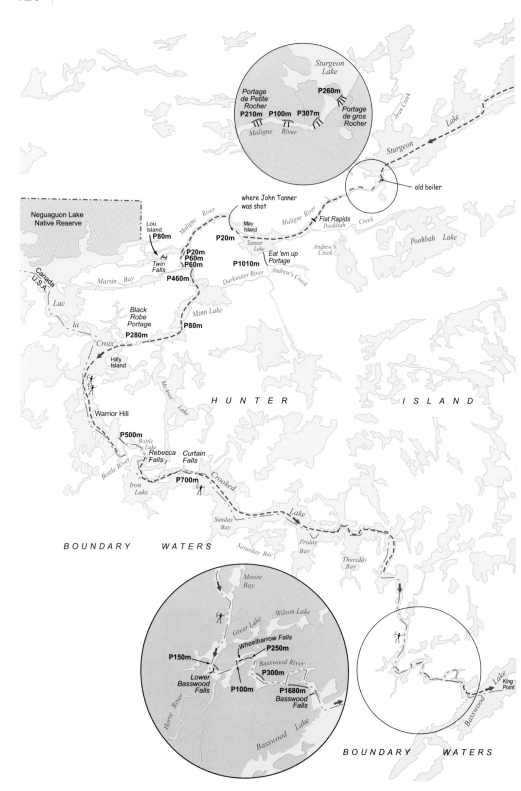

Sturgeon Lake

Portage de Petite Rocher
P210m P100m P307m
Portage de gros Rocher

Maligne River

P260m

Jean Creek

Sturgeon Lake

Sturgeon

old boiler

where John Tanner was shot

Maligne River

Flat Rapids
Poohbah Creek

Poohbah Lake

Neguaguon Lake Native Reserve

Lou Island
P80m

May Island

P20m

Tanner Lake

Eat 'em up Portage

Andrew's Creek

Maligne River

Twin Falls

P20m
P60m
P60m

P1010m

Andrew's Creek

P460m

Darkwater River

Canada U.S.A.

Martin Bay

Lac

la

Black Robe Portage

Minn Lake

Croix

P280m

P80m

Hilly Island

McAree Lake

H U N T E R   I S L A N D

Warrior Hill

P500m

Bottle Lake

Rebecca Falls

Curtain Falls

Bottle River

P700m

Iron Lake

Crooked Lake

Sunday Bay

Friday Bay

Thursday Bay

B O U N D A R Y   W A T E R S

Saturday Bay

Moose Bay

Wilson Lake

Greer Lake

Wheelbarrow Falls

P150m

P250m

Basswood River

Lower Basswood Falls

P300m

P100m

P1680m
Basswood Falls

Horse River

Basswood Lake

Lake

King Point

Basswood

B O U N D A R Y   W A T E R S

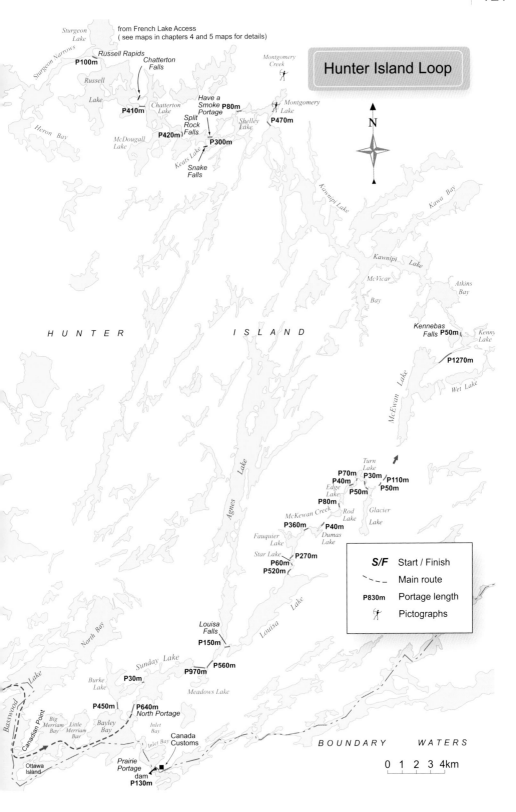

Sturgeon
Lake

from French Lake Access
(see maps in chapters 4 and 5 maps for details)

Sturgeon Narrows

Russell Rapids
P100m

Chatterton
Falls

Montgomery
Creek

Hunter Island Loop

Russell
Lake

P410m

Chatterton
Lake

Have a
Smoke
Portage **P80m**

Montgomery
Lake

P470m

Heron Bay

McDougall
Lake

P420m

Split
Rock
Falls

P300m

Shelley
Lake

Keats Lake

Snake
Falls

N

Kawnipi Lake

Kawa Bay

H U N T E R

I S L A N D

McVicar

Bay

Kawnipi Lake

Atkins
Bay

Kennebas
Falls **P50m**

Kenny
Lake

P1270m

Wet Lake

Agnes

Lake

McEwan Lake

Turn
Lake

P70m **P30m** **P110m**
P40m
Edge **P50m** **P50m**
Lake
P80m

Rod
Lake

Glacier
Lake

McKewan Creek

P360m **P40m**

Fauquier
Lake

Dumas
Lake

Star Lake **P270m**
P60m
P520m

Louisa

Lake

Louisa
Falls

P150m

Louisa

S/F	Start / Finish
- - -	Main route
P830m	Portage length
🏃	Pictographs

North Bay

Sunday Lake

P560m

P970m

Burke
Lake

P30m

Meadows Lake

Basswood Lake

Canadian Point

P450m

Big
Merriam
Bay

Little
Merriam
Bay

Bayley
Bay

P640m
North Portage

Inlet
Bay

Inlet Bay

Canada
Customs

B O U N D A R Y   W A T E R S

Ottawa
Island

Prairie
Portage
dam
P130m

0 1 2 3 4km

In 1823 Tanner and his family traveled up the Maligne River on their way to Sault Ste. Marie, where the children would attend a "white" school. His wife was opposed to Tanner's intentions and secretly planned to have her brother shoot him en route. Tanner wrote: "I had taken off my coat, and I was with great effort pushing up my canoe against the current [Tanner rapids] which compelled me to keep very near the shore, when the discharge of a gun at my side arrested my progress. I heard a bullet whistle past my head, and felt my side touched, at the same instant that the paddle fell from my right hand, and the hand itself dropped powerless to my side."

Of course, this is where the story gets interesting. Poor John Tanner knew nothing of his wife's intentions, or that after the encounter she and her brother had headed back toward Lac la Croix with the children, leaving her husband for dead. Tanner was more concerned over what would happen to his wife and children than about his own wound. The bullet had shattered his right arm and nearly reached the lung, lodging itself under the breastbone. Making it worse, there was a strand of poisoned deer sinew attached to the ball.

Tanner suffered for two nights before being rescued by a group of Hudson's Bay Company voyageurs who happened to be paddling downstream on their way to the Red River. The voyageurs brought Tanner to the fort at Rainy Lake, where he was cared for; that is, until one of the agents who believed him to be "one of those worthless white men who remain in the Indian country from indolence and for the sake of marrying squaws" kicked him out of the fort and forced him to take care of his own wounds.

It took him well over a year to gain back his strength, and it was a few years more before Tanner made it to Sault Ste. Marie. Here, he worked as an interpreter for Henry Schoolcraft — and was eventually accused of murdering Schoolcraft's youngest brother, James. Again, poor John Tanner found himself in the wrong place at the wrong time. He wasn't the murderer. The man responsible was Bryand Tilden Jr., ironically the officer in charge of the soldiers ordered to hunt down Tanner for the murder. Tanner escaped but disappeared, never to be seen again. A skeleton later discovered in a swamp near Sault Ste. Marie was thought to be that of John Tanner. The bones were those of a man who had possibly committed suicide.

What a unique twist of fate. After being kidnapped, living as a Native for over 30 years, being shot, rescued, and then being harshly dismissed by his rescuers, Tanner returned to his white society only to be banished once again. He was labeled the "White Indian," an outcast, a man who was neither savage nor civilized. Because he was accused of murder and escaped into the woods, the name "John Tanner" became synonymous with the bogeyman, and parents used it to keep their children from wandering off. At the same time, however, Tanner's life story took on legendary status. His troubled life became one of the great fascina-

The Maligne River is a beautiful waterway for paddling.

tions of the nineteenth century, especially after Edwin James recorded it in a book entitled *A Narrative of the Captivity and Adventures of John Tanner*, published in 1827. It became a minor classic and was used by educators as a way to depict Native life. The story was also published as a children's book, *Grey Hawk: Life and Adventures,* and later as a Canadian school reader, *John Tanner: Captive Boy Wanderer of the Border Lands*. These stories were read by everyone except for poor John Tanner; he couldn't read.

Andy and I made camp on Tanner Lake, just upstream from Tanner Rapids, the spot where John Tanner was shot.

The Maligne River (Maligne is French for "bad") is a beautiful waterway to paddle. Our morning began with an hour's paddle across what remained of Sturgeon Lake. Then we took on Portage de gros Rocher ("big boulder"), the first portage, a flat 52-rod (286 yd/260 m) trail to the right of some rapids. The take-out is a safe distance from the drop and has an old boiler from a tug used by the first settlers heading west across Sturgeon Lake. It's an easy carry, and the only worry is a giant patch of poison ivy midway across the trail. Another portage, 61 rods (335 yd/307 m), also on the right (and also laden with patches of poison ivy), quickly followed, making use of an old logging road of the Shelvin Clark Lumber Company, who logged here extensively in 1937 and 1938. An easy double swift allowed us to drift by some impressive pine rooted along the banks, some of which still have cable scars from when boats were hauled around the fast water during the logging era. Soon after is another swift, with a 20-rod (110 yd/100 m) bush portage on the right used mostly by paddlers heading upstream. It's a clear run to the far right, but you might want to get out and check it out from the portage first. The takeout for the third and final portage of the day, Portage des Petite Rocher ("small boulder"), was just around the bend and again to the right, a 42-rod (230 yd/210 m) trail. Three or four more swift sections continued, all easily navigable, with the biggest being the last, Flat Rapids. Soon we were flushed into Tanner Lake.

On day five of our trip I definitely didn't have the same urgency to get up and out on the water that I had the previous day. Our Tanner Lake campsite was only half a day's travel from Lac la Croix, and I felt incredibly anxious about paddling this huge chunk of water. Lac la Croix is notorious for heavy winds and waves. It's named after Sieur de la Croix, who drowned during Jacques de Noyon's 1688 trip from Fort Frances. His birchbark canoe overturned while he and his companions were crossing the lake during a storm. All the occupants managed to hold onto the craft except for poor Sieur de la Croix. The lake is even in the shape of a graveyard cross — how spooky is that?

I suggested to Andy that we at least use a "shortcut," the extensive 200-rod (1,100 yd/1010 m) "Eat 'em Up Portage" from the south shore of Tanner Lake. From there we would wind our way through Andrew's Creek to the Darkwater River, then link up with Minn and McAree Lakes. This would eliminate a large portion of paddling on Lac la Croix. Andy would have nothing to do with my plan, however. He had traveled on Lac la Croix a number of times before and promised me it was a wonderful place to paddle. He claimed it was one of the most scenic lakes in all of Quetico.

We compromised and cut out the lake's most northeastern section by using Minn Lake. After portaging 4 rods (22yd/20 m) to the left of Tanner Rapids, on the south side of May Island, we paddled down the Maligne River once again to just before Lou Island. The river forks here and a series of portages would take us to Minn Lake. Before we headed to Minn Lake, however, Andy insisted we at least have a look at Twin Falls, located on the south side of Lou Island, before heading south.

We walked Island Portage, a 15-rod (82 yd/80 m) trail found on the far right of the twin cascades, took a couple of snapshots of this incredible spot, then backtracked to where the river splits towards Minn Lake. Not long after we began navigating the side route, however, I started second-guessing myself. Of the four portages that were supposed take us to Minn Lake, the first two, a 4-rod (22 yd/20 m) trail to the left and a 12-rod (66 yd/60 m) trail to the right, were nonexistent. We lifted over two gigantic beaver dams instead, then we bushwhacked through where a third portage, a 12-rod (66yd/60 m) trail to the left of a set of rapids, was supposed to lead us to Lac la Croix's Martin Bay. The fourth portage

Large white pines, some over 350 years old,
tower over the portages along the Maligne River.

had to be the worst, however. We found it by turning left on Martin's Bay, paddling to the far end of the inlet, then going south. The 92-rod (506 yd/460 m) trail was to the left of a set of rapids and falls flushing into Minn Lake. At least this portage existed, but as it was so overgrown and had muddy sections, in hindsight paddling the full length of Lac la Croix after Twin Falls might have been a better option. The only plus was Minn Lake itself. It was full of pine-clad islands, and we caught some amazing bass by trolling along the far west shore.

The 16-rod (88 yd/80 m) portage connecting the south end of Minn to the top end of McAree Lake was more of a liftover than an actual portage, and the trail connecting McAree with Lac la Croix — measuring 55 rods (302 yd/280 m) and called Black Robe Portage — was a straightforward carry.

The name Black Robe Portage comes from missionary Father Albert Lacombe's meeting with an Ojibwe family here in 1881. Father Lacombe was labeled the "Black Robe Voyageur" for his extensive travel to remote Native villages. In his travels he befriended many influential Native leaders, allowing him to successfully keep the peace between the Cree and Blackfoot, negotiate the development of the Canadian Pacific Railway through Blackfoot territory, and convince Blackfoot leader Crowfoot not to assist the Northwest Rebellion of 1885. He also established many missions but was unsuccessful in Lac la Croix, most likely due to the efforts of Chief Blackstone.

Blackstone, or "Megadaywasin" is a legendary character in the Native history of Quetico. He controlled who traveled through his band's territory, sometimes chasing out gold miners and demanding fees from general travelers making their way through "his" land. He had over 80 warriors under his leadership and had been involved with the Minnesota massacre of 1862. His major campaign was against the Christianization of his people. He asserted that the Ojibwe's beliefs were older than those of the "palefaces" and just as sacred to them as the Bible is to Christians. Due to Blackstone's perseverance, Lac la Croix was one of the few settlements that never had a Catholic mission.

Our campsite that night was on an island southeast of Hilly Island on Lac la Croix. It would have been a nice spot if not for the amount of trash and used toilet paper polluting the back of the site. Obviously we had entered one of the busy spots in the park. In fact, Black Robe Portage is a major access point for canoeists entering Quetico from the United States. Most of the paddlers we saw were being towed across from Crane Lake. Some were even brought in by jetboat or floatplane. We had been paddling for five full days and to now encounter such large groups of paddlers just starting out on their journeys was strange. The only saving grace was that Andy was right about the scenic splendor of Lac la Croix. It definitely is one of Quetico's most beautiful lakes, as befits its original Ojibwe name, Zhingwaako ("lake surrounded by big pine").

We took advantage of an early morning calm on Lac la Croix and pushed off from our island site before 6:00 A.M. We kept close to the eastern shoreline, not only to stay in Canada (the United States boundary runs straight down the middle of the lake) but also because we wanted to check out two historically significant sites: Lac la Croix's Native pictographs and Warrior Hill.

The rock paintings are spread out along two massive cliff faces just three miles (5 km) from our previous campsite, south of Coleman Island's southwestern end. The most striking paintings in the first cluster of pictographs are of moose. There's also a series of animal tracks leading away from a man with braided hair, sitting and smoking a pipe. Then, on a second slab of granite, separated from the first pictograph by a crack in the rock, is another smoker, sitting with exposed genitals. And to the left of the male figure, "L R 1781" has been chipped away in the rock.

Further south is another piece of flat granite with two more panels. The first is a man carrying a spear, below him is a caribou or elk, above that is a stick figure under a dome-shape structure, and scattered throughout are a number of handprints. The second, just to the south, is made up of a small wolf surrounded by more handprints. Some historians have labeled this grouping of pictographs as the "warrior" panel because of their close proximity to Warrior Hill. This steep chunk of rock is located just over a mile to the south, along the east shore, and is thought to have been either a lookout where the Ojibwe watched for their enemies the Sioux or a hill where young Ojibwe braves raced to the top to test their strength and stamina as a warrior.

We spent a good part of the morning gawking at all the Lac la Croix pictographs, and even spent some time attempting to sprint up to the top of Warrior Hill — with limited success, I might add. It was noon before we paddled the full length of Lac la Croix and crossed over the extremely mud-filled 100-rod (550 yd/500 m) portage to Bottle Lake.

A short stretch along the Bottle River linked us up with Iron Lake. Before we moved on to Crooked Lake we took a side trip to view Rebecca Falls on the north shore. This magnificent cascade plunges 23 feet (8 m) into McAree Lake. To check out the falls we approached the central island just above the drop and made use of a bush trail leading to the base of the falls.

At the base of the falls we boiled up a pot of tea and munched on cinnamon bannock that I had cooked that morning, then started our portage to Crooked Lake. The 140-rod (770 yd/700 m) trail is marked to the right of the Curtain Falls and has a steep climb shortly after the takeout. The put-in was also a little too close to the brink of the falls, and we decided to walk further upstream before pushing off. There are a number of side trails along the portage, and the 30-foot (10 m) Curtain Falls is even more impressive than Rebecca.

Campsites were abundant along the right-hand shoreline, but we hadn't purchased a Boundary Waters camping permit prior to our trip, so we had to resort

An average canoeist paddles a thousand strokes an hour. That's 8,000 strokes a day. That means Andy and I paddled close to 130,000 strokes to circumnavigate Hunter Island. Yikes!

to a poor tent site on the Canadian side, directly across from Sunday Bay.

The southern bays of Crooked Lake are labeled after the days of the week that a group of canoeists found themselves lost here (Sunday to Wednesday). Believe me, it's easy to find your self lost here. Several such accounts have been documented, one being that of a group of paddlers from Nebraska who ventured here in 1915: "We started across Crooked Lake at 7 A.M. and were lost three times before noon and as many times after, and camped at night on a river branch of Crooked Lake as totally ignorant of where we were as anyone could be."

Andy and I were confused more than I care to admit while traveling across Crooked Lake the next day. We only became aware of our exact location on the map when we approached Table Rock, a historic campsite used by the early fur-traders and marked by a giant slab of granite resting flat along the southern shoreline. Table Rock is also located a short distance from another cluster of Native pictographs, reported to be one of the best in the park.

The rock-painting site also marks the famed "Rock of Arrows" spot first recorded by Alexander Mackenzie in 1793. Mackenzie was the first European to reach the Pacific by traveling overland by canoe and on foot. Mapmaker David Thompson noted the location in 1797. But the best description was by boundary commissioner Joseph Delafield. While traveling west to Crooked Lake in 1823, Delafield wrote:

A narrow strait with high granitic ridges on the sides and of deep water leads us to Crooked Lake. In this strait, and on the left side just before emerging into the lake, is a high perpendicular granite cliff rendered famous by the circumstances of its having in a fissure of the rock between 20 & 30 feet from the water a number of arrows, said to have been shot there by a war party of the Sioux when on an excursion against Sauters or Chippewas. The party had advanced thus far and, not finding an enemy, shot their arrows in the fissure as well to show that they had been there, as to convince them of their deadly aim. The fissure presents an opening of two inches, and there may be seen still the feather ends of about twenty arrows driven nearly to the end."

The Sioux and Ojibwe battled one another in Quetico until 1736, when the Ojibwe finally forced the Sioux to move to the western plains. This was also the same year a Sioux war party massacred 21 French traders, including La Verendrye's son, Jean Baptiste, and Jesuit father Jean Pierre Aulneau. La Verendrye was the first European explorer to set up a trade system with the Natives in the area, and the first to record a route through Quetico, but some of his trading practices proved unacceptable to local tribes. To express their disapproval, a group of Sioux braves attacked La Verendrye's voyageurs on an island in Lake of the Woods, decapitating the men, wrapping the heads in beaver skins, and arranging them in a council circle.

It was past 4:00 P.M. by the time we reached the first of a series of portages leading to Basswood Lake. However, it stays light well past 10:00 P.M. in June, so we made a silly decision to try and keep going all the way to Basswood. The portages weren't altogether difficult.

The first, to the left of Lower Basswood Falls, measured only 30 rods (165 yd/150 m) and had a slight incline right after the takeout. The second had two choices: a 50-rod (275 yd/250 m) trail to the left of the main cascade, titled Wheelbarrow Falls, or a 20-rod (110 yd/100 m) portage to the extreme left, beside a side chute along the north shore. We took the shorter of the two trails. The third had a portage on both sides of the falls, each measuring 60 rods (330 yd/300 m). We stayed to the Canadian (left) side of the river. And the last carry, titled Horse Portage, was a long but flat 334-rod (1,837 yd/1680 m) trail to the right of Upper Basswood Falls. By the time we began carrying across Horse Portage, however, we were completely exhausted. We changed our minds about making it all the way to Basswood by the end of the first portage. The problem was, every time we went to make camp we found the site already occupied. This is one busy part of Quetico and as a rule if you don't stop around 3:00 in the afternoon to look for a spot to camp, then you'll never find one. It was 9:30 P.M. when we found ourselves stopping three-quarters of the way across Horse Portage and simply pitching the tent right on the trail.

We were two very bedraggled canoeists who had chosen a horrible, buggy spot to camp after an extremely long day, but it was kind of fitting that we stayed overnight on Horse Portage. This trail has real significance to both American and Canadian paddlers. It was here in 1952 that a group of gentlemen canoeists, who the media later dubbed "The Voyageurs," met with their future leader, Sigurd Olson. The initial group had formed the year before during an Ottawa dinner party at which three Canadians and three foreign diplomats planned a short canoe trip down Quebec's Gastineau River. The trip was such a success that the organizer, Eric Morse (author of *The Freshwater Saga*), began planning more trips to retrace Canada's historic waterways. Hunter Island was the first on the list, and Morse contacted Olson, an expert guide for Quetico at the time, to help organize the trip. Olson only met the group on Horse Portage at the completion of their loop but later joined them on countless other adventures, most of which were to remote parts of the far north.

The Horse Portage rendezvous was the start of a lifelong friendship between kindred spirits, but Olson also had an alternative motive for being there when the group arrived. He was in the process of pushing for legislation for joint protection of Quetico and what is now called the Boundary Waters Canoe Area Wilderness. The problem, of course, was that his strategy for creating a new management plan for the 14,000-square-mile (22,530 km²) Rainy Lake watershed included 9,000 square miles (14,500 km²) of Canada. Olson was immediately ridiculed by Chamber of Commerce groups in northwestern Ontario, who believed the idea was just an American proposal to make tourists dollars at Canada's expense. Olson knew he needed positive Canadian publicity, and his newfound friendship with "The Voyageurs" would do just that. That meeting on Horse Portage marked the beginning of what is now titled the Quetico–Superior Wilderness.

That night, while camped out in the middle of Horse Portage, we celebrated the accomplishments of "The Voyageurs" by doing exactly what they did each night at camp; we read aloud a quote that dealt directly with wilderness values. I chose the group's favorite. It was from group member Omond Solandt's mother: "I often feel the need to go camping in the woods. It irons the wrinkles out of my soul."

Most of day seven of our trip was spent battling wind on Basswood Lake. The lake has such a volume and breadth of scale to it that once a strong wind begins to ruffle its surface, the immense body of water takes forever to calm itself. With our attention more on inching our way forward, and at times even just keeping the canoe upright, we had to ignore any plans of visiting the many historical sites along Basswood, including searching for a French fur-trading post reported in David Thompson's journals and the remains of two of the first ranger cabins for Quetico, constructed on King's Point and Cabin 16 Island.

Progress seemed slow at first, but eventually we checked the map and realized the mileage was adding up. We spent our time on the water talking sporadically, re-telling stories of past trips and sharing dreams of places we've yet to paddle. Most of the time, however, was spent gawking at the scenery as we floated along. Halfway across, our ability to paddle in heavy winds required little thought: paddle two strokes forward, brace for an oncoming big wave, then paddle two strokes forward and brace again. Our shoulders were less sore from the strain of each stroke, and we developed a rhythm that was actually relaxing.

By late afternoon we had made it to the entrance to Basswood's Inlet Bay. Not far ahead was Prairie Portage, a 25-rod (138 yd/130 m) trail marking Quetico's most southern access point. From there a series of lakes running straight along the border of the U.S and Canada would link us to Saganaga Lake, where the two waterways split to form Hunter Island. And once at Saganaga the route turned northwest, towards Kawnipi Lake, and back towards Pickerel Lake. The problem was, however, we noticed a line-up of canoeists waiting to use Prairie Portage, and we weren't too thrilled about dealing with crowds again. We were also worried that if we continued east along the major route without an overnight camping permit for the Boundary Waters Country Area Wilderness, we would get stuck again looking for a spot to set up the tent. Andy recommended we backtrack a little ways, portage in to Sunday Lake, and then head northeast to McEwen Lake and Kawnipi Lakes. That would definitely take us away from one of most the crowded areas of the park, but it would also eliminate some of the most scenic and historically significant places en route. For example, Knife Lake is a gorgeous spot and comes complete with a quarter-mile hiking trail to the top of Thunder Point and a visit to Dorothy Molter's Isles of Pines. Until her death in 1986, Dorothy was a legendary figure for thousands of canoeists who knew her as the "Rootbeer Lady" and who stopped by her island home for a bottle of homemade root beer.

We saw another large group of canoeists heading towards Prairie Portage, making a total of 12 canoes and 17 kayaks gathered at the takeout. We decided on the shortcut.

There are two ways to reach Sunday Lake from Basswood's Bayley Bay. The first is to take an easy 90-rod (495 yd/450 m) portage from the top end of Bayley Bay in to Burke Lake and then turn east to a quick liftover beside a small creek. The second is a 127-rod (700 yd/640 m) trail called the North Portage that begins from Bayley Bay's northeastern Sunday Bay. Andy and I took the North Portage, thinking it would save time, which it did, but we had an uphill battle most of the way across, so the moment we paddled out into Sunday Lake we called it day and made camp on the first island to our right.

Fortunately the wind had changed direction by morning, and we were able to race the full length of Sunday Lake. It was a mixed blessing, since we weren't too keen on what was waiting for us at the other end. A 193-rod (1,062 yd/970 m) portage took us into Meadow Lake, and a 110-rod (605 yd/560 m) portage took us out. The first trail was relatively flat but cursed with lots and lots of mud. The second was shorter but had a much steeper incline with a few ankle-twisting rocks to balance on. The payback, however, was brunch and a swim at Louisa Falls. There was an insanely steep 30-rod (165 yd/150 m) portage to the right of the falls, but once we carried the canoe and gear up to the top, we were able to return to the halfway point and relax in the natural Jacuzzi formed in a glacial bowl below the first drop of the 100-foot (33 m) falls.

The route between Bayley Bay and Agnes Lake can be busy at times, and the Louisa Falls pool is an extremely popular destination for paddlers, but once we began paddling northeast across Louisa Lake we knew that crowds wouldn't be an issue. Louisa is a very large, scenic destination lake, but the route that follows is barely used by canoeists.

The first portage, measuring 103 rods (566 yd/520 m) and leading out of the far northeast end, was overgrown and had seen little traffic. It also happens to be all uphill. We missed the 12-rod (66 yd/60 m) portage to Star Lake completely. It was supposed to be somewhere in a bay to the left. Instead we found a rarely used 12-rod (66 yd/60 m) trail to the left of the creek flowing out of Star Lake. We paddled a twisting channel through the center of a marshy area, and then lifted 4 rods (22 yd/20 m) over and through a giant patch of poison ivy to Star Lake. The third, 54 rods (297 yd/270 m) in to Fauquier, could only be reached by getting out and pulling the canoe up a small creek surrounded by muskeg. A few blowdowns blocked the path, but at least downhill it was all the way.

From Fauquier to Dumas Lake, a spot where the flow of water changes direction, the going got worse. The 72-rod (396 yd/360 m) portage was rocky, narrow and wet, with an abrupt crevasse and patches of poison ivy. The small brook, however, was gorgeous. Crystal clear water flushed over medium-sized boulders covered in vibrant-colored moss; the entire section had a fairyland appearance to it and was a highlight of the day. Then, from the eastern inlet of Dumas, there was more creek paddling; the lakes themselves were mere ponds, but each with a character of its own. The center of the creek bed swayed with lime-green angel hair, and the edges were lined with thick patches of white and yellow lilies, pitcher plants, and the occasional calypso orchids.

As we rounded the first bend in the creek after Dumas Lake, we witnessed a wolf preying on a raven. We heard the commotion first, two ravens screaming, and slowed the canoe. We drifted around the corner in time to see a large timber wolf latch onto one raven's wing while the other bird repeatedly dive-bombed the attacker. The wind wasn't in our favor, but the wolf was so preoccupied with both ravens that we were able to float close to the action. It was like watching a nature documentary unfolding right in front of us.

We took on an 8-rod (44 yd/40 m) portage along the right bank of McEwen

Louisa Falls drops over 100 feet (33 m)
and features its own naturally formed Jacuzzi halfway down.

Creek soon after leaving the wolf-raven incident. Between Rod and Edge Lake there was another short portage to the left, complete with an awkward takeout spot. To get from Edge to Turn Lakes, we first considered walking the section of shallow rapids rather than taking the 8-rod (44 yd/40 m) portage to the left. The takeout was covered in poison ivy. But fallen trees on the far side made the idea impossible, so we tiptoed our way through the poison ivy, walked alongside the creek, then climbed over a slab of granite, trudging on until the waterway deepened enough to be navigable again. The next portage is 14 rods (77 yd/70 m) and found to the right of the creek. It leads directly into Turn Lake and was one of the easiest en route.

The creek became even more weed-choked from here, but we managed to find a way to Glacier Lake by keeping to the center and making use of two more portages to take us around two sections of swift water, the first being an easy 6-rod (33 yd/30 m) trail to the right and the second being a 10-rod (55 yd/50 m) trail also to the right, with the takeout hidden by a large boulder.

Our plan was to reach McKewen Lake by the end of the day, which we could have done by taking two more portages — a 10-rod (55 yd/50 m) trail to the left, which splits after the takeout and either takes you over a steep mound of rock or keeps you close to the creek, and a 22-rod (121 yd/110 m) trail to the right of a shallow, rockbound rapid (you could actually line down this one rather than portage) — followed by a couple more miles of twisting McEwen Creek. Glacier Lake, however, was too perfect to pass up. It was a clear, deep lake surrounded by cliffs and loaded with feisty smallmouth bass. And best of all, no one was there. The lake was so perfect that we made our campsite east of the island, directly in front of a granite bluff. This would be our home for two solid days.

Having a rest day during an extensive trip is a must for canoe trippers. The midway point is the best time for it. You're in too much of a hurry at the beginning, and way too much of a hurry at the end of your trip, but by the midway point, your body and mind are in need of a rest. Our time off was spent brewing an extra pot of coffee in the morning, cooking up extra bannock for lunch, and exploring an unnamed lake to the northeast of Turn Lake, a lake that is off the regular canoe route and that turned out to be full of bass.

There was a slight drizzle on day ten, but it meant there were no winds pushing hard against us as we paddled the expanse of McEwen Lake and then Kawnipi Lake. And we only had two portages to deal with. The first, measuring a lengthy 252-rod (1,386 yd/1270 m) and connecting the northeastern inlet of McEwen Lake to Kenny Lake, wasn't too bad of a walk. It took us under two hours to complete both carries, and most of the steep parts were downhill. The second portage connected Kenny to Kawnipi Lake. It measures less than 10 rods (55 yd/50 m) but was more problematic than the much longer trail. This portage is on the left-hand side of Kennebas Falls, the last drop in what's called the "Falls Chain." The water was high, and the takeout is unnervingly close to the brink of the falls.

The rest of the day was spent paddling effortlessly along the shoreline of Kawnipi Lake, finally moving over to the western shore to check out the two pictograph sites at the entrance to Kawa Bay. The first painting is near the southern entrance to bay, and the second is near the northern entrance. Of the two sites, only the first is easily recognizable. The second, believed to be of Missepishu (the Great Lynx), is far too faded. We located the first panel directly below an obvious crack in the rock face. The pictograph portrayed two (possibly three) Maymaygwayshi sitting in a canoe. The figures had what seemed to be horns on their heads and were sitting in the canoe with their arms bent at their waists. To me, they looked like spirits standing on guard, almost daring you to enter a sacred place, which may make sense since Kawa Bay and the river at the far eastern end (Wawaig River) were part of a well-known Ojibwe travel route.

We camped that night on an island in the center of Kawa Bay, with enough time to catch and clean a few walleye for supper. At this point in the trip, we were down to freeze-dried meals and just a few fingers of rum to wash it down with. Fresh fish was always a welcome change, and mixing the rum with clear tea helped our supply of spirits last a little longer.

We left our Kawnipi Lake campsite just before 9:00 A.M., waiting patiently for the wind to shift and clear the morning rain clouds. We chose to continue north into Montgomery Lake rather than twist around to the southwest to Kahshahpiwi Creek. Either way would have allowed us to continue down the Maligne River, but the Kahshahpiwi route required an 8-rod (44 yd/40 m) portage to either to the left or the right of some rapids that Andy remembered from a previous trip as having a takeout uncomfortably close to the main drop. The Montgomery route had an overgrown 94-rod (517 yd/470 m) portage, with the first section of the trail skirting close to the right of a large, muddy swamp. But Montgomery was by far the better route choice. We had the lake all to ourselves and even took half a day off to explore the out-of-the-way Montgomery Creek pictographs. Sadly, our attempt to locate the paintings failed. Andy and I managed to drag ourselves, and the canoe, up to a small pond, where we searched in vain. When we later talked to the park staff about the route to the Montgomery Creek paintings, they informed us that the pictograph site was quite a ways north of the pond.

The paintings were discovered by local trapper Phil Sawdo, who came upon them while snowshoeing through the area in the winter of 1983. They're isolated, far away from any known navigable route. Two of the three animal symbols depict caribou, and the third, reported to be a moose, could quite possibly be a caribou as well. One of the human figures is armed with a bow and arrow — a rare symbol to find in Quetico. Sawdo believed the paintings marked a spot where hunters ambushed herds of caribou. Woodland caribou were present in the Quetico area up to the 1930s, but if the symbols represent barrenland caribou, it would date the paintings at over a thousand years old.

Andy and I weren't too upset about not getting to see the remote Montgomery Creek paintings, especially because we spotted a rarely viewed pictograph directly below our campsite on Montgomery Lake (the painting, which is of a male stick-figure with an erect penis, was discovered in 1984 by David Ingebrigtsen). We were camped high atop a ridge, on the easternmost section of a small island, north of a large central island and separated by a long section of rock. Both the tent site and the painting were exceptional.

Leaving Montgomery, we headed west. We portaged a quick 16 rods (88 yd/80 m) in to the top end of Shelley Lake, then followed the right-hand shoreline all the way to the 60-rod (330 yd/300 m) Have-a-Smoke Portage. The map showed another route to the south, where a couple of shorter but much steeper portages are marked to the right of what's labeled Snake Falls. Andy and I, however, chose to take the simpler trail and thankfully discovered "Have a Smoke" to be uneventful.

Split Rock Portage was next. It's marked to the right and measures a total 84 rods (462 yd/420 m) if you use the high-water takeout, which you definitely want to do. From there we paddled across Chatterton Lake and carried across

Discovering fresh bear prints beside your tent in the morning can be uplifting but also a little unnerving.

the 82-rod (450 yd/410 m) portage to the south of Chatterton Falls. This trail is about a mile south of the falls, and even though it was the most rugged of the day, it definitely doesn't compare to the nasty trail that's directly beside the falls on the left bank. I've walked that trail before, and it's a great way to view the cascade, but I wouldn't even dream of carrying a canoe across it. Instead, we carried across the portage to the south, then paddled up to the base of Chatterton Falls to have a look.

The remainder of the afternoon was spent paddling across scenic Russell Lake, then flushing down the set of rapids linking Russell with the upper end of Sturgeon Lake (a 20-rod or 110 yd/100 m portage is also located to the left). We decided to camp that night on the very same site we had occupied our second night out. We'd finally come full circle, and from here we only had to retrace our familiar route back to French Lake over the next couple of days. To celebrate, we finished off the remainder of our rum supply.

At dawn I walked down to the shoreline to fill up the coffee pot and noticed bear tracks, prints in the sand that I'm sure weren't there the night before. Nothing on the site had been disturbed. The tracks were in a straight line away from the direction of our food cache. The bear had obviously ignored what our camp had to offer, which wasn't much by this point in the trip.

The interesting part about the event was my reaction. It was the complete opposite of what it would have been if the bear had walked through our camp at the beginning of the trip. I would have definitely felt anxious — terrified, actually. Now I was more upset that we hadn't managed to spot the bruin wandering by. A close encounter with a bear would have been an exciting addition to our trip, not a reason for panic. I liked that feeling, a feeling that by completing the Hunter Island loop, I had become comfortable with these surroundings, a "Quetico regular."

Hunter Island Loop

LENGTH: 12–14 days

PORTAGES: 42

LONGEST PORTAGE: 334 rods (1,837 yd/1680 m)

DIFFICULTY: Intermediate to advanced canoe-tripping skills are required.

ACCESS: French Lake (Dawson Trail Campground) is located at the main campground in the northeast corner of the park, just south off Highway 11. It's a 130-mile (210 km) drive west of Thunder Bay and 24 miles (39 km) east of Atikokan.

ALTERNATIVE ACCESS: This route can be accessed by any entry point in the park. The one we chose is best only if you are a Canadian who doesn't want to cross the border to the US. The best overall entry point, especially if you are entering from the US, is at Saganaga Lake. To reach the public launch on most southerly inlet of Saganaga Lake, take the 56-mile (90 km) Cook County Lake Road (Gunflint Trail Road) to its most northwestern end. The road begins in the town of Grand Marais, Minnesota.

TOPOGRAPHICAL MAPS: 52-B/3, 52-B/4, 52-B/5, 52-B/6, 52-B/11

FISHER MAPS: F-11, F-16, F-17, F-18, F-19, F-23, F-25, F-30

BEYOND QUETICO

OKAY. I KNOW WHAT YOU'RE THINKING: Why did the author only write half the chapters dealing with "Beyond Quetico"? Well, because the people who wrote the other half know more about those areas than I do. Trust me, I did it for your own good.

It was Lynn Cox from Canoe Frontier Outfitters who led me to consider outside help. I'd had the upper Albany River on my list of places to paddle for years and had bugged Lynn frequently for information on the route. Then, as I sat in on one of her talks at the Midwest Mountaineering Show in Minneapolis, I came to realize how silly it was for me to try and write about it when the person who knew all about the river was Lynn herself.

I first met Phil Cotton (a.k.a. "Voyageur") in January 2006 at the annual Wilderness Canoeing Association (WCA) Symposium in Toronto. He was speaking about his efforts to rediscover and reclaim "lost" or abandoned canoe routes in Wabakimi Provincial Park. (A cool thing for me was that his work was inspired in part by my book *A Paddler's Guide to Ontario's Lost Canoe Routes.*) It seems that the first-ever management plan is in the works for this park, which is twice the size of Quetico but with less than five percent of its visitation rate. Phil is concerned that unless these canoe routes are documented and included in the plan as park "values," they'll be lost and forgotten forever. At the conclusion of his WCA presentation, Phil invited volunteers to join him and share the costs of the next season's not-for-profit expeditions. That summer, he organized and led 11 four-person "teams" to continue exploration of the remote and rarely visited region of the park beyond the Ogoki River. Collectively, they spent 87 days clearing and mapping portages and cleaning and recording the locations of campsites. They traveled more than 250 miles (400 km) of canoe routes, which included 131 portages totaling over 6,442 rods (35,433 yd/32,400 m) in length, and visited 74 campsites.

I met Barry Simon (a.k.a. "Boneli") at Canoecopia in Madison, Wisconsin. He participated in one of Phil Cotton's reconnaissance trips in 2005 and enthusiastically volunteered to collaborate with him in developing a series of digital canoe route maps. (If you want to join one of Phil's Wabakimi trips, he can be contacted at pjcotton@tbaytel.net. Barry can be contacted at: wabakimimaps@hotmail.com.)

The other addition to this book is by Scott and Kathy Warner, people whom I believe exemplify true canoe culture. Though we were complete strangers at the time, the Warners mailed me free replacement food barrels after hearing how I'd been robbed of all my gear after a trip. That gesture is typical of most people who

Quetico Park has inspired many paddlers to head further north in search of even wilder places. Mart Tannahill photo

paddle; it's a type of kinship we have with one another. As a retirement adventure, the Warners undertook a 60-day trip in Woodland Caribou Provincial Park and were so moved by that trip that they returned for 65 days to travel the land north of there and visit its seven neighboring First Nations communities. The Woodland Caribou area is an ancient landscape in need of much better protection. The Warners believe the only way to do this is to advertise it to paddlers, let them see first-hand how precious it really is, and in turn they will help guarantee it a better future. Thankfully, that work is beginning to pay off. Recently Woodland Caribou Park was voted as the number one place to paddle *beyond* Quetico. Scott and Kathy's weeklong sampler provides a good introduction to the park.

According to all the paddlers who have graciously added information and stories to this guidebook, the routes that follow represent a small fraction of the countless possibilities. Albany River, Wabakimi and Woodland Caribou are all remote areas to the north of Quetico, where crowds are definitely not an issue. With their remote lakes and infrequent, short portages, these chunks of wilderness are dream destinations for the avid canoeist. Before your trip's end, you'll find yourself poring over maps planning another one.

12 White Otter Lake Route

IN JULY 1998, ALANA AND I SPENT A WEEK paddling the Turtle River, a 100-mile-long (160 km) provincial waterway park located north of Quetico Park and south of the town of Ignace (for a route description, see my book *A Paddler's Guide to the Rivers of Ontario and Quebec*). It was an amazing river journey, one that shouldn't be missed, and one of the highlights was when we paddled across White Otter Lake on the first day out to make a pilgrimage to Jimmy McOuat's (pronounced McQuat) White Otter Castle, one of the North's most mysterious hermitages.

The castle — and White Otter Lake, for that matter — is certainly not as remote as the Turtle River. This 28-by-38-foot (8.5 by 11.5 m) log structure was built by a 60-year-old hermit eight decades ago and has been a local drawing card for years. One of its first visitors was canoeist C.L. Hodson, while working on an article for *Rod and Gun* magazine in 1914: "Mile after mile of rugged shoreline drops behind and then about 2:30 P.M. 'Old Jimmy's Place' quite suddenly slips into view. A hundred yards back from the lake it stands on the edge of a small clearing. In the background are dark pine woods. No one speaks but with one accord the paddlers pause here. Eyes strain. Heartbeats quicken. In the very air is mystery. Almost, we fear to approach this retreat of the wild man. We are intrud-

White Otter Castle is one of the North's most mysterious hermitages.

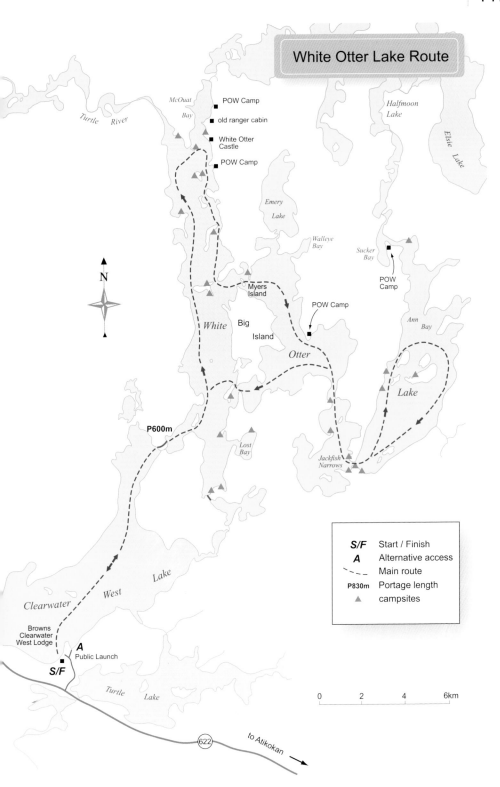

Alana checks out the Native painting that gives Turtle River its name. It's the only pictograph in North America depicting a turtle with a canoe protruding from its back end.

ers — trespassers. Then, slowly, the paddles dip. The bow grates on a strip of sandy beach. Gingerly we step ashore and approach the hermitage."

I felt a little shortchanged, having read Hodson's description of his visit. Sure, the castle is impressive, standing four stories high and built of 200 pine logs averaging 37 feet (11 m) long, but what made Hodson's arrival more exciting than ours was that "Old Jimmy" was home at the time. And, intrigued by all the stories about why the hermit had built the bizarre monument (one of the most romantic involves a mail-order bride who canceled the deal because Jimmy lacked a proper house), Hodson was able to ask the builder himself.

It seems it all had to do with McOuat being falsely accused of throwing a corncob at a bad-tempered schoolmaster (Jimmy's chum had thrown the cob). For some reason, he was never able to forget the curse imposed by his angry schoolmaster: "Jimmy McOuat, ye'll never do any good! Ye'll die in a shack!" Decades later, Jimmy found the accursed prophecy coming true. After gambling his life savings away on a failed gold rush, he found himself living in a shack on the shores of the remote White Otter Lake (then known as Clearwater Lake). "All the time I lived in a shack," Jimmy told Hodson, "I kept thinking: I must build me a house. And so I have. You couldn't call this a shack, could ya?"

In 1918, four years after Hodson's visit, Jimmy McOuat drowned while netting fish in front of his castle. His partially decomposed body, wrapped up in fish netting, was found the next spring by forest rangers and buried beside his beloved wilderness home.

Alana and I have returned to White Otter Lake several times since, but not just to tour Jimmy's castle. The lake itself has much to offer, including a total of 23 Native painting sites, a number of logging camps that once served as a prisoner-of-war camp, and the site of an old ranger station. And because it is approximately 50 square miles (80 km²), with 155 miles (250 km) of shoreline, and countless beaches, islands and rocky-outcrop camping spots, it's a great destination for paddlers, especially those who prefer the kayak over the canoe.

Jimmy's gravesite on White Otter Lake.

White Otter Lake Route

LENGTH: 2–4 days

PORTAGES: 1

LONGEST PORTAGE: 120 rods (656 yd/600 m)

DIFFICULTY: Only novice skills are required, but beware of high winds on the lake.

FEE STRUCTURE: White Otter Lake is part of the unmaintained Turtle River Provincial Park, and at this point no camping fees are required for Canadian citizens. However, non-residents must obtain a Crown land camping permit from the District office.

ACCESS: The best way to access White Otter Lake is to launch at Browns' Clearwater West Lodge on Clearwater West Lake (www.brownsclearwater-lodge.com or 1-807-597-2884). The lodge is reached by driving north of Atikokan on Highway 622 and turning east onto Clear Lake West Road, and then left to Browns Clearwater West Lodge (taking the right fork in the road will also lead you a small public launch area). From here you paddle northeast across Clearwater and locate the 120-rod (656 yd/600 m) portage linking Clearwater with White Otter Lake. The well-used put-in, located along the top right of the northern inlet of Clearwater Lake, even has a boat shuttle service operated by the lodge.

ALTERNATIVE ACCESS: A public launch area is also available on Clearwater West Lake, located by following the right fork on Clearwater West Road.

TOPOGRAPHICAL MAPS: 52 F/8, 52 G/5, 52 G/4, & 52 F/1

The Ontario Parks have also produced an excellent CANOE ROUTE MAP for the entire Turtle River Waterway Park.

13 Wabakimi's Center of the Universe Route

IT WAS ONTARIO PARK PLANNER NANCY SCOTT who first got me intrigued with the idea of paddling in Wabakimi Provincial Park, located 185 miles (300 km) north of Thunder Bay. The fact that the park measures almost 2.5 million acres (one million hectares) in size and contains over 1,240 miles (2000 km) of canoe trails was enough to catch my interest. But it was Nancy's story of eccentric inventor Wendell Beckwith, who lived alone for 20 years on Wabakimi's Whitewater Lake to devote his life to "pure" research, which finally convinced me to visit this massive chunk of solitude.

Joining me on the pilgrimage to the Beckwith site was film producer Kip Spidell. It was our first trip together. He was convinced that if he followed a bumbling canoehead like me through the wilderness for eight days, he'd get enough good film footage to make the trip worthwhile.

Mercifully, Nancy had agreed to tag along as guide. Not only did she know the exact whereabouts of Wendell's hermitage on Whitewater Lake, but she also knew the locations of all the unmarked portages and campsites along the way — a bonus for any group traveling in such a remote park, where woodland caribou far outnumber canoeists.

The three possible ways to access the park are by road, rail and floatplane. The road is obviously the cheapest route, but not necessarily the best overall. It's a relatively easy drive to the launch site on Caribou Lake, 7.5 miles (12 km) north of Armstrong via the Armstrong Road (Highway 527) and then Caribou Lake Road. But the full-day's paddle across the expanse of Caribou Lake to the actual park boundary can be a real bore, not to mention extremely hazardous should the wind pick up.

However, keeping to the train schedule can also be a pain at times, and the flights in and out can be costly. So after looking over all the options, our group finally decided on a combination plan. We would access the south section by train (check Via Rail Canada for schedules and fees), fly out of Mattice Lake Outfitters on Whitewater Lake by way of Don Elliot's Wabakimi Air Service, and then have Don shuttle us back to the train station in Armstrong.

Since Kip and I both live in southern Ontario, we planned to take the Via Rail service out of Toronto's Union Station. If all went well, we would meet up with Nancy 24 hours later in the Armstrong station and continue east for another 24 miles (39 km) and be dropped off at the designed access point, Shultz's Trail, at the south end of Onamakawash Lake.

Thinking back, our plan went surprisingly well, though Kip and I managed to bump into a handful of not-so-friendly commuters while portaging down Front

*Three major rivers must be paddled
before reaching the expanse of Wabakimi's Whitewater Lake.*

Street during rush hour, and I managed to break an overhead light while carrying through the main foyer of Union Station (which, for some reason, caused a power surge throughout the entire building), and a broken axle on the train caused us to be six hours late for meeting Nancy in Armstrong.

Under the watchful eyes of the tourists we had befriended in the Budd car, the three of us waved our goodbyes, dragged our gear down a steep gravel embankment, then paddled off into the Wabakimi wilderness.

An hour and a half later, we had paddled to the northeast bay of Onamakawash Lake and flushed ourselves down the first rapid of the Lookout River (a 20-rod/110 yd/100 m portage is found to the left), all the time being pursued by a massive black storm cloud.

Nancy had warned us about the severity of the storms in Wabakimi, but Kip and I thought we could get in at least the first day of paddling before we would have to deal with one. Suddenly, the black squall caught up to us. There was no buildup, no prelude, just the smack of hard rain, strong winds, and a lather of whitecaps. We pushed for the second stretch of rapids, hastily made camp at the takeout for the 10-rod (55 yd/50 m) portage on the left bank, and then watched from under a sagging rain tarp as the storm moved across the sky.

For our second day out, we pushed off from camp early, attempting to film our own version of the Bob Izumi fishing show at the base of the rapids, with no luck, of course. By 8:00 A.M. we were heading downriver.

The Lookout River was the first of three rivers we planned to travel to reach Whitewater Lake. And thinking back, it also happened to be my favorite. Of the series of five rapids between our first night's camp and Spring Lake, only the fourth could be safely run. But all the portages were extremely short: 20 rods (110 yd/100 m) on the left, 20 rods (110 yd/100 m) and 8 rods (44 yd/40 m) on the right, a possible liftover on the left, and 30 rods (164 yd/150 m) on the left, and the scenery along the intimate little stream was absolutely breathtaking. Even the last portage of the day — a 180-rod (984 yd/900 m) trail connecting Spring Lake with Smoothrock Lake — was a pleasure to walk. Aptly named Fantasia Portage for its fairyland appearance, and rumored to be the most scenic portage in the North, the trail led us through a stand of pine, spruce and birch, all rooted in a thick carpet of caribou moss, bunchberries and knuckle-size blueberries. (Take note that a heavy snowfall the following year felled a number of trees along this portage.)

Smoothrock Lake (named for its cluster of islands scoured smooth by passing glaciers) was a different story, however. Almost the entire 20 miles (30 km) of shoreline still display the effects of a fire that went through the area in the early 1980s. Since wildfires play an integral part in the lifecycle of the boreal forest, they are not always suppressed. This management practice ensures a vital habitat for the park's scattered herds of woodland caribou, as well as all other boreal species. For canoeists looking for a place to camp, however, the landscape can seem inhospitable. Around 6:00 P.M., just minutes before the nightly storm moved in, we finally found a suitable spot on a tiny knob of rock situated in the center of the lake.

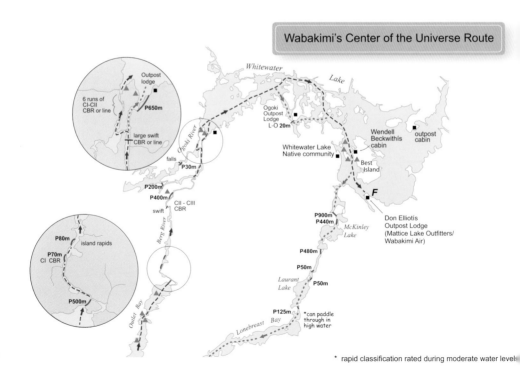

Wabakimi's Center of the Universe Route

* rapid classification rated during moderate water level

It was amazingly calm the next day when we began our six-hour crossing of Smoothrock Lake. On such a large lake, we were grateful for the lack of wind, but the payback was an intense heat, reaching 90 degrees Fahrenheit (32°C) by 8:00 A.M. We kept close to the shoreline most of the day, searching for a bit of shade. The previous fire had scarred most of the trees along the shore, however, and escaping the direct sun soon became a lost cause. To make matters worse, we could smell smoke from a distant fire, probably started by a lightning strike during the previous night's storm. A thin veil of haze hung low over the lake and breathing became increasingly difficult throughout the day.

By late afternoon, as we entered Smoothrock's Outlet Bay (the second of three channels that lead northward out of the lake), a soft breeze was helping clear the air of smoke. The shift in wind also indicated that another evening storm was brewing. In the distance, we spotted anvil-shaped clouds moving our way. This time they had a green hue to them, something Nancy seemed quite concerned about, so we immediately headed for shore.

Of course, as luck would have it, we were quickly chased off by thousands of biting red ants (it was like some kind of horror flick), and we made haste toward the next rocky point. The second we pulled up onshore, the storm hit. And what a storm it was! The temperature dropped to freezing in a matter of minutes; hail the size of marbles smacked down hard, leaving dimple marks on the overturned canoes; and a gale-force wind brought trees down all around us.

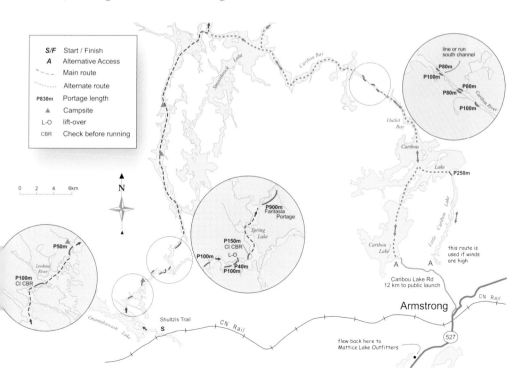

The calm after the storm.

It was a horrifying experience. It only lasted five minutes, but as we crept out to the water's edge to check the damage done to our two canoes, we realized how lucky we were to have made it through the storm without serious injury. The original point we had pulled up on was now littered with uprooted trees. It was obvious that if we had stayed there, all three of us might well have been crushed to death. It was a humbling revelation.

We had only an hour's paddling on Smoothrock Lake the next morning before we reached the portage leading to the Berg River. The trail was only 100 rods (547 yd/500 m) long, but this section of forest had been burned over recently, and it took us another hour to haul our gear and canoes through the charred debris. Once on the Berg, however, we made quick progress. We easily ran the first set of rapids, even though a short 14-rod (77 yd/70 m) portage was found on the left. The second set, Island Rapids, had to be portaged. But the 16-rod (87 yd/80 m) trail along the left bank was an easy carry. Once we reached the third set, we decided to call it an early day and camped along the 80-rod 437 yd/400 m) portage, also found on the left.

Here Kip spent some time shooting whitewater scenes for his film by having me paddle down the Class II-III rapids over half a dozen times. I didn't mind the job, as the water levels were up and most of the dangerous rocks were well submerged. The only thing I had to watch out for was billowing waves at the beginning and end of the run, which became a problem after Kip duct-taped his camera and tripod to the back end of my canoe. With the extra weight strapped to the stern, each maneuver became a balancing act. And since Kip forgot the waterproof casing for the camera, he constantly reminded me that a dump in the rapids would be a costly mistake.

The morning of day five saw us finish the remainder of the Berg River, and we entered the Ogoki River before noon. This was the last of the three rivers en route and also happened to be the largest and least exciting to paddle. It's slow and meandering in this section, with only one section of quick water, and that can be easily run or lined down. We also began seeing fishermen from the neighboring lodges. (Wabakimi Provincial Park has 7 main lodges and 40 fly-in outpost camps.) So, rather than take the regular 130-rod (710 yd/650 m) portage to the right of where the main section of the Ogoki empties into Whitewater Lake, we made a sharp left turn just over half a mile (1 km) up from the takeout and navigated a small side stream instead.

There were no portages and we had to wade, line and blindly run down a series of rock-strewn rapids. But in a way, the narrow outlet was a far better introduction to Whitewater Lake. And there to greet us at the entrance to Wendell Beckwith's "Center of the Universe" was our first woodland caribou. The encounter lasted only a couple of seconds, but even the brief glimpse we had was well worth it. Throughout Wabakimi, the second-largest park in the province, only 300 of these elusive creatures remain.

Caribou once ranged as far south as Lake Nipissing, but they were eventually pushed further north by settlement and logging. Because they are an extremely vulnerable species that depend greatly on isolation for their survival, their future viability lies in part here in Wabakimi. Established in 1983, the park was expanded six-fold in 1997, primarily to provide for the protection of the caribou. But is this enough? According to the Ministry of Natural Resources Regional Planning Biologist for Northwestern Ontario, Glen Hooper, it's not even close to enough. Hooper admits that the park provides a vast and very significant chunk of habitat for this important population, but warns that it is neither large enough nor remote enough to sustain caribou on its own.

However, the park superintendent continues to promote the high number of hunting and fishing lodges throughout the expansion area. Most canoeists traveling in the park feel ambivalent about the camps. They don't seem to fit the "wilderness experience" concept; on the other hand, they can be extremely handy as links to the outside world. Occasionally, trippers use them as a meeting place for floatplanes or to pick up extra supplies. Others have had to use them in emergency situations.

Our group was no different. Before our trip to Wabakimi, the park superintendent had offered to have Walter, the interior park warden, meet us at the lodge situated at the mouth of the Ogoki River. From here he would give us a tow across to the Wendell Beckwith site on Best Island, situated on the far southeastern bay of Whitewater Lake, a distance of approximately 12 miles (20 km).

In a way, it was a bit of a cop-out to accept the free ride, but Walter was also a member of a small group of aboriginal people who had lived on Whitewater Lake during Wendell Beckwith's time here, and Kip thought that an interview with him would help his film a great deal. So early the next morning, our group gathered on the lodge's dock and waited for Walter to show. The following day we were still waiting. At 3:00 A.M. of the second day, the same day we had scheduled a plane to pick us up at another lodge just south of Best Island, we were forced to find our own way across. Of course, when we finally arrived, Walter was there to greet us. After many years of traveling in the North, I've come to realize that schedules are not the same up here as they are down south. I also believe that far too many of us "visitors" fail to see the importance of not being in such a hurry, and that we should not enter the bush without a good understanding of "bush time." This didn't seem to help me curb my frustration, and it took some time before I could excuse Walter's tardiness.

To help ease the situation, we went off to explore the Beckwith site. Walter gave us a tour of the three cabins and a couple of storage sheds that remain on the island, all connected by a flagstone walkway and surrounded by a decorative cedar-rail fence. Each structure was designed perfectly and every shingle and floorboard cut precisely. Elaborate carvings adorned all three entranceways, and pieces of the inventor's scientific contraptions and scores of Ojibwe artifacts were scattered about. Walter even pointed out part of a homemade telescope he had found down by the beach, and sections of Beckwith's "lunar gun" (a device constructed to compute and predict lunar cycles and eclipses) resting beside one of the storage sheds.

In 1955, after producing at least 14 patents, most of them for the Parker Pen Company, Beckwith left his wife and five children behind in Wisconsin and began his solitary life on Whitewater. The cabins didn't actually belong to Beckwith. Harry Wirth, a San Francisco architect and developer, used the island site as a retreat and hired Wendell as a caretaker.

Beckwith wasn't the only one to choose Wabakimi as a wilderness retreat. From 1977 to 1982, Joel and Mary Crokham trapped and homesteaded on nearby Wabakimi Lake, where they raised their two young children, Sarah and Jason. And in the spring of 1994, Les Stroud and Sue Jamison lived "on what the bush provided" on Goldsborough Lake while working on their film *Snowshoes and Solitude*. Even Zabe MacEachren, a graduate of Lakehead University's Outdoor Recreation program, attempted to overwinter at Wendell's place. After a close encounter with a pack of wolves, however, she decided to walk back out to Armstrong in February, just five months after she began her sojourn.

Wendell Beckwith was surely the most unique historical resident. During his time here, the eccentric inventor worked on various theories, ranging from the idea that the mathematical term "Pi" recurred constantly in nature to the idea that

In 1978 Wendell Beckwith built an environmental masterpiece he nicknamed the "Snail."

Whitewater Lake was in complete triangulation with the Great Pyramids and Stonehenge (hence his "Center of the Universe" premise).

Obviously, this was no simple hermitage built by a man trying to escape the civilized world; it was a laboratory, observation post and research station.

The first cabin Walter showed us was a split-level building known as the guest-house, or Rose's Cabin. The modest structure is thought to have been the living quarters for Rose Chaltry while she visited Wendell Beckwith. Rose was Harry Wirth's secretary, who came to know Wendell and supported him financially after he had a major dispute with Wirth in 1975.

The main cabin, the only structure not completely designed by Beckwith, came with its own icebox, which was lowered underground to keep food from spoiling, and a sizeable homemade birchbark canoe lashed to the south wall. This was where Wendell stayed at first, but he soon found it far too showy and impractical. The massive stone fireplace was especially ineffective at heating the cabin during the long winter months, and he became concerned about his reduced hours of research.

By 1978, he had completed construction on the "Snail," a circular cabin built directly into the side of a hill. The structure was far more heat-efficient, especially with a skylight centered above a sunken stove, equipped with rotating conical shield to direct the heat and a pivoting chimney to allow for maximum draft. It was an environmental masterpiece, and touring through the unconventional earth-cabin was the highlight of the trip for me.

To end our visit to Best Island, Walter walked us down to the small beach near the Snail and showed us where Wendell died of a heart attack back in 1980, alone but content. It was then that we noticed yet another storm brewing overhead. Since the lodge where we had planned for Don Elliot's air service to pick us up was another 2.5 miles (4 km) south of Best Island, we made the call to leave immediately.

Before departing, we rushed around the island to complete our different tasks. Nancy prepared the canoes, Kip finished filming the interior of the cabins, and I went off to sign our names in the registry book resting on the table inside the Snail. It was here that I saw an entry from Wendell's daughter, Laura, dated August 6, 1997: "Very proud to be the daughter of such a man. Wish everyone could have seen his 'domain' as it was while he was alive. By all accounts he was an exceptional and extraordinary man whose ideas and theories we may never comprehend — but we can all admire what he built here and the life he fashioned for himself. I last hugged him on the beach here — and I feel his presence still. Goodbye again, Dad."

Beckwith's vision — to have a community of researchers living on the island in their own Snails, "cleaning their minds of the mental paraphernalia in the outside world" — may not have been a bad idea. Truly, he was not some mad scientist, but rather a renaissance man who designed a perfect life for himself in this wild place called Wabakimi.

Wabakimi's Center of the Universe Route

LENGTH: 8–10 days

NUMBER OF PORTAGES: 12

LONGEST PORTAGE: 180 rods (984 yd/900 m), Fantasia Portage

DIFFICULTY: Whitewater experience is not an absolute necessity, but intermediate tripping skills are required due to the remoteness of the route.

ACCESS: Train access from the Armstrong station heads west for 24 miles (39 km) to a designated drop off point — Shultz's Trail — at the south end of Onamakawash Lake. Mattice Lake Outfitters then picks you up by bushplane on Whitewater Lake and takes you back to their base near Armstrong and drives you back to town.

ALTERNATIVE ACCESS: Smoothrock Lake can be reached by paddling across Caribou Lake (use Little Caribou if the winds are too heavy) to Outlet Bay and then down the Caribou River to Caribou Bay. Once you've followed the regular route to Whitewater Lake's Best Island, you can loop back to Smoothrock Lake by heading south through McKinley Lake, Laurent Lake and Smoothrock's Lonebreast Bay. From here, you backtrack on the Caribou River and Caribou Lake.

TOPOGRAPHICAL MAPS: 52 I/6, 52 I/11, 52 I/12, 52 I/14 & 53 I/5

14 Upper Albany River Route

Lynn Cox

IT WAS A TREAT TO BE HEADING OUT onto the Albany River again in June, this time with old friends and return guests from Wisconsin. They were all keen anglers, which meant we'd be traveling at a much more leisurely pace than normal. The Upper Albany was the perfect choice, giving us the opportunity to have a relaxing paddle and still have plenty of time to try our luck for northern pike, walleye and especially the wily brook trout.

So the foursome — Bill, Jessie (Bill's grandson), Ron and Mike — headed out from the drop off (at Cedar Rapids, the eastern shore of Osnaburgh Lake) located about 25 miles (40 km) south of the town of Pickle Lake, on Highway 599. My paddling partner, Alana, and I were to join them at a spot farther downstream the following day after being dropped off by air.

We found them about 7 miles (12 km) east on Osnaburgh Lake just prior to Rogers Point, at a lovely campsite at the top of the middle channel where the lake empties back into the river over a series of ledges. We waited at the bottom while they ran the rapids with little difficulty and avoided the estimated 100-rod (547 yd/500 m) portage located on river left of the center channel. Judging by the number of trees across the trail, I guessed most paddlers either ran or lined these rapids.

I had explored the north channel on earlier trips and found a lovely rock garden to pick through; a fine choice if one is trying to avoid the rapids, but a poor choice in low water conditions. It's wise to check this channel out in higher con-

Prime campsite along the upper reaches of the Albany River. Jerry Nichols photo

ditions since the river is notorious for its wildly fluctuating levels. The dams located between Lake St. Joseph and Osnaburgh Lake keep water back throughout the dry season but are opened up in July, when there has been more rain and the lake levels are healthy. This translates to a river that offers a different experience each time you head out.

Past experience on this river reminded me how drastic its water conditions can be. Five years earlier, I'd guided a Women's Whitewater Learning Adventure group on the Upper Albany. We were dropped by air along a stretch of river northwest of Achapi Lake, where the Wisconsin group's previous trip had ended. I remember the look our pilot, Sean Bell, gave us as we slid our canoes off the plane's floats and into the turbid water. We couldn't get to shore to unload because there wasn't any. No shore, just flowing water that extended up into the trees. Even in this supposedly slow section of river, the water had that sickening swirling and flowing look that one sees on TV footage of flooded streets in disaster zones following hurricanes or flash floods. I could tell Sean was happy to be the pilot and not the guide — especially to a bunch of paddlers with limited experience (some group members hadn't even camped before).

Well, we not only endured that trip, we reveled in the glory of the rapids and falls. Higher risks provided us with higher personal rewards; a feeling I discovered en route that I longed to experience all over again. Point is, the river is a new adventure every time you paddle it.

Now I was back, it was June, and our drop-off day on the river. Alana and I had skipped paddling Osnaburgh Lake — too bad, really, since it is full of islands, beaches and flat rocks. It's a lovely paddle that gets folks "geared up" and in the paddling rhythm before they enter the river proper. There are plenty of campsites available for groups, no matter when they are dropped off at Cedar Rapids.

Our group spent the sun-filled day fishing and exploring the north channel, then running a couple of easy rapids and a more technical run filled with half-submerged boulders, just before the Albany empties into Atikokwam Lake (also known as Caribou Lodge Lake). We stayed at the beach site in the northeast corner where the lake turns back into river. This is a lovely spot that offers a west-facing campsite and a number of tent sites in the bush along the shore.

The next morning, we spotted the first of many moose on this trip. A mother and two calves who swam so closely together it was difficult to tell them apart, with their tiny moose heads and big ears skimming the water's surface. After drifting for some time to watch the moose family meandering through the marshy area, we headed downstream to York Boat Portage. A nice 100-rod (547 yd/ 500 m) trail around a significant drop and a series of falls on river left takes you to the bottom of the outwash rapids. The alternative trail, found on the large-scale maps, still exists and measures 120 rods (656 yd/600 m). We discovered this trail by paddling to the end and walking back up to the start, where the willow-choked

The difficulty of each rapid found along the Albany depends greatly on the water level of the river. Mart Tannahill photo

entrance was just a stone's throw deeper into the bay from the portage we had taken. It's said that the Hudson's Bay Company brought their York boats all the way up from Fort Albany to Osnaburgh House trading post on Lake St. Joseph. The trail is wide and runs straight through the bush, which made me feel the York boat story may well be true.

Next came three consecutive rapids, including a large gaping whirlpool. This yawning hole opens and closes in rhythm with the flow of the river, revealing its menacing maw for an impossibly long time, only to snap shut and blanket the area with calm water. Quite a sight and easily missed as one zips along the treadmill of swift-moving water. We began the run by hugging the right shore, then over to the center to catch an eddy on the left. Our options from there were to either line along the left shore or to back ferry over to the right shore, keeping with the fast current and hopefully avoiding the whirlpool. We chose the second option,and narrowly missed the whirlpool just before we took a quick eddy stop on river right, a maneuver that was needed for us to line up with the last section — a fairly easy but fast run that took us in an arc along river right, into the deeper water, then back over to the center of the river, where we found shelter from the current behind the large, rocky island.

Our day ended at the base of the last rapid, a straight run through a deep V (careful not to smack into the large, flat rock that sits dead center in the V). We cooked up the pickerel we had caught in the deep channel below the rapids and

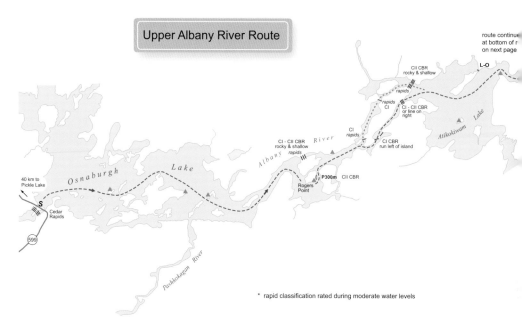

route continues
at bottom of r
on next page

* rapid classification rated during moderate water levels

settled into our tents for the night. The next day we would reach the 34-foot (10 m) Kagami Falls, a favorite camping spot for a layover day.

The section leading up to falls can be wild and wooly. We opted to line and eddy hop most of this section since, for me at least, the price to pay if you tipped was too high. Bill and Jessie ran the section to the tiny eddy at the top of the falls. The first portage takeout, located at the back of a pointy bay on river right was already choked with rocks (in lower water it would become a boulder field), so we decided to head for the second take-out. I remembered the eddy at the top of the falls to be tiny, but I knew it was there. From this tiny eddy, on river right at the top of the falls, there is a 120-rod (656yd/600 m) portage.

Bill and Jessie decided to run this section, hugging river right. About halfway down they spun sideways and grabbed the gunnels, a harbinger of a pinned canoe to come. I even turned to Alana and said, "Watch! This is how to pin a canoe." But Bill and Jessie proved me wrong. Both paddlers, with lightning speed and fox-like agility grabbed the gunnels yes, but only to gain purchase on the canoe so they could propel their bodies into the air to execute a full 180-degree turn and drop soundly down into their seats, facing the wrong way. They scooped up their paddles and miraculously paddled back out into the main current. We cheered with delight and hoped they survived as they disappeared around the corner. The line was not too difficult, and once around to the top of the falls we found Bill and Jessie, smiling, pleased with their success.

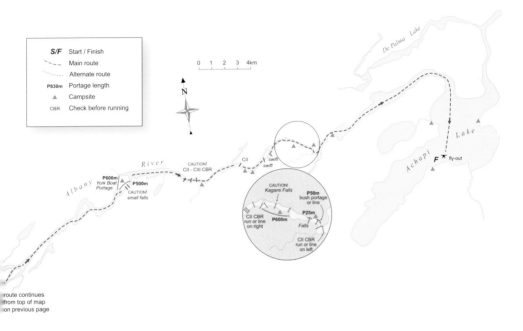

The trail is pretty good; as folks pass through they cut their way, leaving only a few obstacles to climb over. Ron had made "a wrong turn at Albuquerque" and headed back up to the first take-out. Once he realized his mistake, he claimed to enjoy the extra exercise from carrying the canoe twice as far as needed. That was his story and he was sticking to it. The roomy campsite here overlooks the falls and is located just short of the put-in.

The stretch between Kagami and Achapi Lake is short, but traveling it takes a bit of time. There is another falls/drop just a short paddle from the Kagami portage put-in. This is where, several years earlier, while guiding the Canadian Armed Forces, Jerry — teacher, friend, guide and great paddling partner — and I got out to scout a possible lift over around the falls. In order to avoid the short 5-rod (27 yd/25 m) portage, on river left, we thought it would be less time-consuming to slide our fully loaded canoes over the small trickle of water that followed the left shore. Gravity would provide the biggest advantage we said, but as we scanned the route we spotted two canoes precariously adrift at the top lip of the falls. There had been some disagreement, and the paddlers we were guiding had entered into a bit of shoving match, resulting in the canoes' detachment from the safety of the shoreline take-out. Jerry called up, and as they turned their heads to respond, their eyes took in the full impact of the situation. Terror was not the expression, as these were soldiers; instead we saw firm concentration and determination. At this point, one canoe darted sideways and jammed itself at the head of the rivulet we were inspecting, but in the second canoe, the other paddlers took on the impossible task of paddling upstream and, to their thinking, out of danger.

Paddling across the lip of the falls, these paddlers tried with all their might to move upstream, but all that happened was a successful sideways ferry away from the 15-foot (5 m) falls and toward an even more terrifying drop to a re-circulating hole on river right. It was apparent a new course of action was required. It was time to paddle backwards. Many a river paddler has had to negotiate the river from the backward seat. Almost like riding the Go Train in Toronto, looking at where you have been instead of where you are going; most exhilarating in the right circumstances, but in times of survival, disorienting and extremely challenging. Jerry called out to the two struggling canoeists, "Paddle backwards!" They looked up, nodded affirmation to the order, and proceeded to back-paddle. No hesitation. No "Are you nuts?" Just "Yes, sir" and away they went.

We watched in awe as the canoe ran a perfect line down the falls, in the best possible stream, on a 45-degree angle into the boiling water below. Next would come the canoe "dig" as the stern entered the "seam" where the force of the falling water met the upstream flow of the re-circulating water. It was going to be ugly, but Jerry and I were ready with our throw bags, ready to fish out the paddlers before they got sucked under the strong current.

Instead, the canoe darted down the falls and punched into the water only to be spit straight up into the air again. Their canoe popped up like a cork and astonishingly landed right-side up, albeit full of water. Amazed at their brush with death, the paddlers paddled off across the bay. Jerry and I fell down laughing, partly from the hilarity of the scene, and partly from nervous relief that no one was harmed.

The remainder of the trip seemed to pale in comparison. We ran all the rapids with little effort, since a feat such as the one just witnessed was pretty hard to beat. The next section to Achapi Lake involves lining along the left shore or running a ledge and series of rapids around to the swift water to the marshy area to the north of the lake. We caught pickerel while trolling with the Army here. So, on our June trip, Alana and I stopped off at a ledge by a pretty little grassy campsite where the rocks formed a perfect sitting bench by the fire pit, to try our hand at fishing. It was midday, with the hot sun overhead, the worst time to catch fish. We laughed as we caught one after another. Alana was tickled to see the fish grab her rubber worm on a lead-head jig in about four feet (just over a meter) of water. We had no problem catching enough to eat for supper. We finally tired of having to catch and release so many fish and decided to move on.

Upon leaving the marshy section of river we spotted two young cow moose grazing in the shallow water. Our upwind approach gave us the advantage of paddling an entire arc around their location before they sensed our presence. One appeared to stand watch while the other ate, switching roles every so often.

Achapi Lake has a flatter terrain than the upper portion of the river but also offers some incredible beach campsites. Lorne Morrow photo

There is a very nice beach campsite at the mouth of the river where Achapi turns back into the Albany River, but on this trip it was occupied by other campers. This was not a problem since the deluxe beach site a mere 2 miles (3.5 km) to the south was available. In the late afternoon sun we headed off to make our camp along the shore of the expansive beach. This would be our pick-up point the following day, a perfect place for the floatplane to land, with alternative docking locations depending on the wind direction.

That evening, after cleaning and eating our fish, we settled into our beds with the faint flicker of northern lights as the backdrop. In the heat and in my laziness, we had set up the tent close to the water's edge. It just seemed so far to walk up the beach into the edge of the bush to carry all our equipment so we plopped right down on the sand where we had landed. As I drifted off to sleep, my brain reminded me that we had cleaned the fish on the shore and that maybe there would be the smell of fish on the sand and that...*zzzzz.* Later I was slowly aroused from a deep, deep sleep by the sound of something heavy walking through the water, a mere paddle's length or so from my head. My first thought was BEAR! I sat bolt upright on my mattress and exclaimed, "What the?!" I suppose the crunch of my air mattress (down-filled that is) and the sound of my loud human voice startled the poor animal into a full defensive retreat into the water. From my view through the tent screen, I had the delight of watching a mother moose and her young charge stampede into the shallow bay silhouetted in front of a curtain of green and white northern lights.

Once I returned to breathing normally, I was able to hear the sounds of the cow moose gently urging her child to safety on the far shore over my heartbeat. I laid back in my bed and gave a silent prayer of thanks for such a wonderful trip.

The continuation of the Albany from Achapi to Miminiska Lake is a journey that offers a perfect mix of lake and river travel: few formal portages, gorgeous campsites on rock ledges and beaches, fantastic fishing and plentiful wildlife-viewing opportunities. The typical canoe party will take 7 days to accomplish this 9-mile (150 km) stretch of river. The drop-off is by road shuttle and pick-up can take place anywhere along the river where the aircraft can land, providing alternative pick up locations and thereby reducing stress to meet the "final destination" for pick up. Affordable, accessible and still pristine, this far northern river has experienced relatively few visitors. Longer trips can go as far as the community of Eabametoong First Nation (Fort Hope), or Ogoki Post First Nation (Martin Falls) or even as far as Fort Albany on the coast of James Bay. The entire trip of 245 miles (394 km) takes the average paddlers a month to do. There are two commercial lodges along the way, on Miminiska and on Makokibatan Lake. Both operations are owned and operated by the Liddle family and based in North Bay (Liddle's Fishing Adventures).

Upper Albany River Route

LENGTH: 4–5 days (Achapi Lake pick up), 7 days (Snowflake, Patte or Miminiska Lake pick up), 10–12 days (Miminiska or Fort Hope) or longer (28 days to Fort Albany).

PORTAGES: 5 to Achapi Lake

LONGEST PORTAGE: 120 rods (656 yd/600 m)

DIFFICULTY: Depends on water level. Typically the river is a perfect trip for those who possess solid paddling skills and plenty of experience in remote wilderness and who want to try their hand at paddling in moving water. All paddlers should take a moving water paddling course prior to heading out on the river. For experienced river-trippers, this route provides some challenging whitewater sections. Novice paddlers should travel with a guide or paddle with experienced moving-water trippers.

ACCESS: Road access from Highway 599 (Rat Rapids is the northwest corner access for Osnaburgh Lake, but most folks paddle east from the Cedar Rapids drop).

ALTERNATIVE ACCESS: Alternative access from Pashkokagan Lake northeast along the Pashkokagan River to join the Albany at Atikokwam Lake. As well, flights are available to any spot along the river (some folks put in where their trip ended the previous year, making the Albany a continuous route spread across several years) from Pickle Lake or from Armstrong.

TOPOGRAPHICAL MAPS: 52 O/1, 52 P/4, 52 P/5, 52 P/6, 52 P/7, 52 P/10, 52 P/11

Although the Albany River is designated as a Waterway Provincial Park, it is currently "non-operating" therefore no Ontario Parks Camping Permits are required.

15 Wabakimi's Palisade River Route

Phil Cotton

OUR TWO TANDEM CANOES BOBBED IDLY in the shelter of an island on Burntrock Lake, in the remote northwest portion of Wabakimi Provincial Park, as we scanned the horizon and listened intently. One canoe was loaded with gear; the other was empty. Suddenly, I sat upright, and hearing the faint, distant drone of an approaching aircraft, I announced, "Incoming!"

A DeHavilland Beaver floatplane appeared on the horizon, swooped by in a low pass, banked sharply, came around on final approach and gracefully touched down near our waiting canoes. We took up our paddles and raced toward the aircraft as it taxied to a stop. As we approached, the pilot swung down onto the starboard float, retrieved an anchor and rope from a rear compartment, tied the rope to a cleat on the float, set the anchor and called out cheerfully, "Morning, Phil!" From my position in the stern of the empty canoe, I responded, "Hi, Don!"

The plane's passengers peered out of the aircraft windows and tried to take in what was happening. This was the rendezvous they had so eagerly anticipated since last winter when they had signed up for one of a series of Wabakimi canoe trips.

Don Elliott, owner of Wabakimi Air Ltd., opened the rear door. The first passenger stepped gingerly down the ladder onto the float, turned and declared, "I'm Barry Simon. You must be Uncle Phil!"

"I am," I nodded. "Welcome to Wabakimi!"

Barry was ushered forward on the float to replace my bow paddler; the other two passengers disembarked onto the opposite float and exchanged positions with the paddlers from the other canoe. Everyone was talking excitedly, introducing themselves and asking questions: "Seen any moose?" "How was the fishing?"

In the midst of all this confusion, Don began passing cargo from the plane's hold for me to stow in my empty canoe. That done, he slid across to the other side of the plane to receive the contents of the loaded canoe. When that was done, Don asked, "Who's going to be co-pilot?" One of the departing paddlers clambered up the ladder and squirmed into the front seat while the others took up places on the rear bench seat.

Final farewells and promises to stay in touch were cut short when Don closed the passenger door and went forward to haul in the anchor. As he stowed it, he handed me my provincial park interior camping permit and asked, "Where will you be next Saturday?"

I handed him my completed Float Plan form detailing the planned route and replied, "Kenoji Lake, on the island just north of the outflow of the Ogoki River."

"OK!" Don said, "See you there!" and swung up into the pilot's seat.

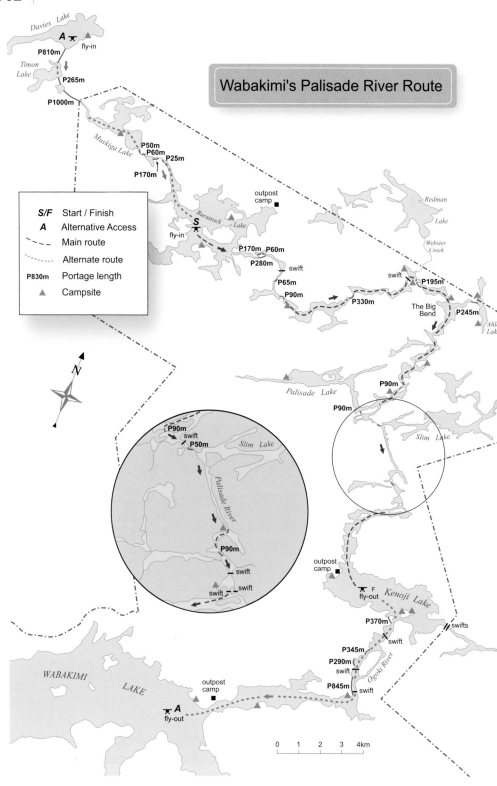

Wabakimi's Palisade River Route

S/F   Start / Finish
A   Alternative Access
— —   Main route
······   Alternate route
P830m   Portage length
▲   Campsite

Davies Lake

A   fly-in
P810m
Timon Lake
P265m
P1000m
Muskiga Lake
P50m
P60m
P25m
P170m
Burntrock Lake
outpost camp
S
fly-in
P170m   **P60m**
P280m
swift
P65m
P90m
P330m
swift
P195m
The Big Bend
P245m
Redman Lake
Webster Creek
Ahle Lake

Palisade Lake
P90m
P90m
Slim Lake

N

P90m
swift
P50m
Slim Lake
Palisade River
P90m
swift
swift   swift

outpost camp
F
fly-out
Kenoji Lake
P370m
swift
P345m
P290m
swift
P845m
swift
Ogoki River
swifts

WABAKIMI LAKE
outpost camp
A
fly-out

0   1   2   3   4km

We untied the canoes and pulled away. Once we were out of reach of any prop wash, Don started the engine. With a whine, a cough and a burst of blue smoke, it came to life, the prop began turning, and the Beaver slowly taxied away.

We waved as the plane took off and disappeared over the horizon towards the air base at Mattice Lake, near Armstrong, then we turned toward the nearby south shore, where our erected tents could be seen. Conversation was minimal as each member of my new team concentrated on adjusting to strange canoes and paddling partners. I watched closely, assessing individual strokes, for I'd soon have to decide who was capable of assuming command of the other canoe.

We landed, unloaded and hauled personal gear, supplies and food up to the campsite. There, we finally had a chance to exchange greetings, and I could match faces to the names that I'd memorized months ago. Despite the fact none of us had met before, we felt comfortable in each other's company, having exchanged many e-mails and phone calls over the past months in preparation for this adventure. I began a briefing session that included a review of safety procedures, familiarization with the equipment, as well as orientation to our location and the route we were to follow over the next week.

This was not your run-of-the-mill wilderness canoe trip. These people had volunteered to participate in a reconnaissance of one of the park's canoe routes that would involve clearing portages, documenting their locations and measuring their lengths. Existing and potential campsites would be visited and inspected, and the condition and location of each carefully recorded. Sightings of large animals, birds of prey and fur-bearing mammals, and signs of human activity or occupancy of the area (e.g., pictographs) would also be noted. All of this data would eventually be turned over to Ontario Parks in an attempt to help planners develop the park's first Management Plan.

Our route would lead us from Burntrock Lake down the Palisade River to Kenoji Lake. As we would encounter at least 20 portages and as many campsites, it's not surprising that a route normally traveled in 2-3 days by competent trippers would take us a full week. Side trips to explore new routes and links to existing routes would also occupy much of our time.

The Palisade River route is historically significant and quite popular. To the west, it connects via Muskiga Lake over the height of land to Davies Lake in the Albany River drainage system. The Palisade River lies in the Ogoki River basin and links via that waterway to two of the park's largest water bodies: Whitewater Lake, to the east, and Wabakimi Lake, to the south. Webster, Corky and Travale Creeks and the Slim River are its main tributaries.

The Palisade River is aptly named. Its granite cliffs tower over the river, reaching ever higher downstream towards Kenoji Lake. Wildlife sightings are common, as are unsubstantiated reports of pictographs. The "drop and pool" nature of the river is typical of area waterways. Each elevation drop usually entails a portage to bypass unrunnable rapids or a falls. Despite the fact that the Palisade drops 52 feet (16 m) between Burntrock and Kenoji Lakes, there's no perceptible current, making travel more like a leisurely float trip. It's an easy haul upstream, too!

That afternoon, after organizing our supplies and enjoying a light lunch, we packed the sharp edges (axes, buck saws, brush axes and Sierra saws) and set off to explore the Upper Palisade River in search of an alternate route to Davies Lake.

Paddling west across Burntrock Lake, we entered this rarely traveled waterway and soon encountered our first obstacle, a set of rapids reduced to a trickle by low water conditions. It didn't take long to find an old blaze on the shoreline, proof positive that we weren't the first to visit this area.

The 34-rod (186 yd/ 170 m) portage, located directly after a short liftover, was in a total disrepair and took several hours to clear and measure. We portaged our canoes and gear and continued a short distance only to encounter another portage, this one a mere 12 rods (65 yd/ 60 m). By the time we'd dealt with it, it was time to return to our campsite. Another trip would have to be planned to press further upstream on this route. Besides, everyone was eager to wet a line in the hopes of adding fresh fish to the supper menu.

Our angling attempts proved successful. Everyone lucked out, and we enjoyed a tasty and filling fish fry. Pickerel (walleye) and northern pike abound in the tea-colored waters of Wabakimi. There are no bass and only a few coldwater lakes that provide suitable habitat for lake trout. Speckled trout can be found in small creeks, especially in the Albany River and Lake Nipigon watersheds.

While I cooked supper, my crew relaxed, writing journals, reading or reviewing digital photos taken during their flight. After supper, campfire conversation inevitably drifted towards the subject that had brought us together: the future of the park. The thorny issues that reflect conflicting interests of different user groups were discussed, and while no consensus was reached, the sharing of information and opinions helped everyone appreciate that development of a long-term plan for the management of the park would be a daunting task.

That night, the northern lights danced across the sky. Our elevated campsite was a perfect viewing platform. One of our crew had never seen the aurora borealis in all its majesty and sat in awe of its constantly changing shapes and colors. We soon retired to our tents, tired after a long first day. Lulled by the rhythmic lapping of the waves along the shore and by the distant, plaintive call of a loon, each of us dropped off into a deep, satisfying sleep.

The next morning, under sunny skies, we struck east across Burntrock Lake towards the outflow of the Palisade River. The lake's name accurately reflects its condition — much of the shoreline was ravaged years ago by a forest fire. Plant growth had been burned down to the bare rock of the Canadian Shield.

The scene sparked a lively debate about the role of fire in the boreal forest and the merits of human intervention to suppress a natural process that encour-

Phil and Barry check out the next day's misadventure. Phil Cotton photo

ages regeneration of certain species, such as the jackpine.

The exit from Burntrock Lake involves a pair of portages (34 and 12 rods/ 186 and 65 yd/170 m and 60 m) that follow the Palisade River or a single 55-rod (306 yd/280 m) portage overland to the next navigable section of the river. We spent the morning clearing and measuring each of them. A cached boat and outboard motor at the foot of the first river portage gave rise to a vigorous discussion about the practice of extending the angling range of a remote outpost camp beyond the lake on which it's located.

Beyond the portages, the Palisade River turns south through a shallow swift that can be bypassed on the left shore via a 13-rod (71 yd/65 m) portage. At the foot of the swift, the river turns abruptly left, making the run difficult but not impossible in high water. We cleared and measured the portage and continued downstream.

Just below the swift, the river turns east again, and we were confronted with a significant drop culminating in a pretty cascade, complete with a 18-rod (98 yd/ 90 m) portage on the left. Studying the shoreline, we tried to imagine what it would look like during spring break-up. The pool below promised to be an exciting angling opportunity, so we camped on the opposite island. We were not disappointed.

Barry Simon is one of the dozens of volunteers dedicated to saving the network of canoe routes throughout Wabakimi. Phil Cotton photo

As we sat within earshot of the tumbling rapids, Barry turned to me and asked, "Why exactly are you doing this, Phil?"

I answered with a well-rehearsed response: "I want to make Wabakimi more inviting and user-friendly by improving its canoe routes, particularly those that have been lost or abandoned and fallen into disrepair. Preservation of these park values will make backcountry travel safer, disperse visitor traffic over a wider area, lessen the impact of human activity on the park environs, and enhance users' experiences."

I continued, "There's no direct road access to Wabakimi. It's surrounded by Crown land that must be crossed to access the park. That these Crown lands lie in five MNR (Ministry of Natural Resources) districts makes efforts to protect the park's access routes complicated. I want Ontario Parks to recognize these canoe routes as an integral component of the park's values and include prescriptions for their protection and preservation in the management plan. The first step must be reconnaissance of these canoe routes to verify they actually exist and to document them in detail."

Day Two brought cloudy weather and high winds, which did not affect our determination to press on. The narrow confines of the Palisade River offered us protection. I reminded my crew of Don Elliott's favorite prediction: "Wait five minutes and the weather in Wabakimi will change." We did and it poured!

The river turned northeast, and we discovered an island not marked on Provincial Series Topographical Map 52 I/13. At the end of this section, we encountered an interesting set of connected portages, totaling 65 rods (360 yd/330 m). The first 10-rod (55 yd/50 m) trail bypasses a short set of rapids that curve to the right around a small island on which we found some magnificent old-growth cedar. A narrow channel on the right side of the island can be waded when water levels permit.

Both channels around the island lead to a pool that the second portage (25 rods/136 yd/125 m) follows along the right shore. We chose to paddle across the pool, but at the north end of the pool, the river was blocked by debris, forcing us to use the third portage (30 rods/170 yd/155 m).

To our delight, the portage ended beside a picturesque falls below which the current offered us the opportunity to hone our ferrying skills. I posed one of my favorite, enigmatic questions to my crew, "Which end of the canoe leads when executing a ferry?" Responses varied and after sorting out the answer, we practiced what we'd learned.

After a short northeast haul, the Palisade River narrows, creating a shallow swift when water levels are high. We camped at the top of the next portage (40 rods/213 yd/195 m) in order to mount a side trip the next day to check out Webster Creek upstream to Redman Lake. The five portages in this short section hadn't been checked since last year and needed to be re-visited.

It's said that at any given time, as much as 30 percent of the boreal forest is horizontal. Blowdowns are common, making regular portage maintenance necessary. In October 2001, a brief but violent wind left a band of destruction stretching across the southern part of the park, evidence of which can still be seen.

Day Four found us breaking camp in anticipation of a busy day. We crossed the portage and soon arrived at "The Big Bend" where the Palisade River turns sharply south towards Kenoji Lake. From here, one can portage 50 rods (268 yd/245 m) into Ahleen Lake and follow Corky Creek downstream to the Slim River, which flows into the Palisade River. We continued downstream to the 18-rod (98 yd/90 m) portage that leads into a widening of the river large enough to be dignified with its own name. Palisade Lake stretches a good distance west.

The Palisade River exits Palisade Lake through a narrow gorge. Care must be taken in approaching the upper landing of the 18-rod (98 yd/90 m) portage during high water, as it lies very close to the mouth of the gorge. The unwary paddler could easily be swept into a roaring cauldron of Class V rapids. We paddled to a lovely campsite at the west end of Palisade Lake, taking care to avoid crushing the delicate pink lady's-slipper orchids throughout the campsite.

The next day, while exploring Travale Creek in search of a route west, we found evidence of previous occupancy and repaired the first two portages (25 and

18 rods/137 and 98 yd/125 and 90 m). Further exploration of this route would have to wait until next year.

Day Six found us returning to the Palisade River via an alternate, more direct, 18-rod (98 yd/90 m) portage. Below it, we passed through a series of swifts and a set of rapids that require careful lining or the use of a 10-rod (55 yd/50 m) portage during spring runoff. Below the rapids, the Slim River joins the Palisade River with little fanfare. Only one more portage (18-rod (98 yd/90 m) and a pair of swifts lay between us and Kenoji Lake.

We checked the final portage, measuring 74 rods (405 yd/370 m), ran the rapids, negotiated the final swift in the river's right (west) channel, and set up camp at the mouth of the Palisade River. From there, we backtracked to inspect the first portage of the route that links to Scrag Lake via Little Scrag Lake. Entering the bay in search of the landing, Barry spotted a small black bear on the shore. We watched it for a few minutes until it caught our scent and bolted into the bush.

"Have you seen many bears this year?" Barry asked.

"That's the first bear I've ever seen in the park, and I've been here since '82," I replied. "Wabakimi doesn't have a bear problem because it doesn't have a people problem — not yet anyway!"

"What about caribou?" Barry asked.

"Ah, that's a different story. The main reason the park was created in '83 and doubled in size in '97 was to protect their natural habitat. Unlike their tundra relatives that travel in large herds, the primary survival technique of woodland caribou is isolation. In the summer, they travel alone, moving silently through the boreal forest like ghosts. They're rarely seen, but their presence is evident by the droppings we find along portage trails. I've only seen three in the 25 years I've been coming here."

Day Seven: our last full day! A freshening breeze pushed us southeast across Kenoji Lake toward our final campsite on a large island just north of where the Ogoki River enters from Wabakimi Lake. From there, we investigated the 70-rod (377 yd/345 m) portage that bypasses the first of four sets of rapids.

That evening, as I notated my map, Barry turned to me and asked, "How long will this project of yours take?"

"Oh," I mused, "at this rate, probably two or three more summers at least."

"But it's a finite undertaking!" Barry exclaimed. "There are only so many canoe routes in the park. What'll you do when you're done?"

"The routes we discover will need regular maintenance or they'll simply be lost again," I replied. "Ultimately, I hope our collective efforts will result in the creation of a non-profit 'Friends of Wabakimi' organization, whose volunteers can continue the work we've initiated. This can't happen until the management plan is developed and approved. Until then, with the able assistance and enthusiastic support of volunteers like you, I'll go on organizing and leading reconnaissance trips to explore the park and document its values."

"I'd like to help" Barry offered. "I could develop the route maps."

"But you live near Milwaukee, and I live in Thunder Bay."

"Ever heard of the internet?" Barry asked. "Well, we met each other over the Net. Why not use it to continue the work? We can exchange map files by email. It'll be a unique 'hands across the border' collaboration."

"You're on!" I said, shaking his hand. "I'll take any help I can get!"

The next day, we rose early, cleaned equipment and packed gear and supplies to be sent out on the rendezvous flight. As we sat in our canoes waiting for the plane, we reminisced about our experience in this vast wilderness area, somewhat overwhelmed by the size of the park and the scope of our undertaking.

"Where to now, Phil?" Barry asked.

"The Ogoki River," I replied. "It's the crossroads of the park."

Our conversation was interrupted by the drone of Don Elliott's Beaver as it appeared over the horizon.

"Incoming!" I announced. "It's time to go!"

Wabakimi's Palisade River Route

LENGTH: 5–7 days
[Allowing for weather and side trips.]

PORTAGES:
7–8, depending on water levels

LONGEST PORTAGE:
55-rod (306 yd/280 m)

DIFFICULTY:
Intermediate tripping skills are required
ACCESS: Floatplane to Burntrock Lake

ALTERNATIVE ACCESS: None

TOPOGRAPHICAL MAPS:
52 I/13 (Burntrock Lake)

16 Woodland Caribou Sampler Route

Kathy and Scott Warner

OVER A 60-DAY "WELCOME TO RETIREMENT" expedition in north-western Ontario, my wife Kathy and I stepped back in time as we wove our way through over 500 miles (800 km) of pristine Ojibwe waterways set inside the 1.2-million-acre (450,000 ha) boreal landscape known as Woodland Caribou Park. Woodland Caribou is nestled against Manitoba's Atikaki Wilderness Park, and both parks form part of an immense piece of Precambrian Shield wilderness nominated in 2004 for a UNESCO World Heritage Site designation. Primarily a pool and drop system of lakes and rivers flowing east to west and draining into Lake Winnipeg, the park offers endless routes for the avid paddler.

It's common to find yourself alone out here. On average, less then a thousand paddlers visit the park per season. You'll find no designated campsites, no ranger stations, and no roads. Interior park access is by canoe or floatplane. Wildfires are also commonplace; an element necessary to help regenerate the boreal forest. But a recent burn can also leave portages blocked by downed trees and at times even obliterate all signs of a portage. Park staff endeavor to brush-out and blaze each portage at least once every four years, more frequently in areas of natural calamity, but being equipped to rely on your own skills, tools and sound judgment will go a long way toward ensuring your safety out here. You'll need good wilderness skills, proficiency with map and compass, and good equipment.

Woodland Caribou Park is rich in cultural history and bio-diversity. Glacial granite cliffs, whose troughs spawn the headwaters of one of Canada's Heritage Rivers, the Bloodvein, showcase an immense natural gallery of shamanistic vision sites. Our paddles dipped quietly as we passed numerous red-ochre pictographs revealing ancient images that fueled our imaginations and transported us back hundreds of years.

In retrospect, I realize now that we were on a spiritual journey. Our goal was to travel softly, peacefully and become one with the land and its inhabitants; to understand the nature of our interconnectedness; to live it and feel it. We followed the native tradition of leaving tobacco offerings to the Great Spirit where we felt it appropriate, and the rewards came daily: a sense of inclusion as the moose and caribou showed us no fear, as loons, otters and beavers entertained us with their comical, playful antics; a sense of continuity as my steps were inexplicably led off the path directly to a set of decaying, handcarved paddles, a testament to travelers from another time; a sense of protection as raging winds and lightning leveled trees around us yet we emerged unscathed; and a sense of humility as we recognized that, aside from all our cautious planning and preparedness,

Scott and Kathy Warner introduced themselves to Woodland Caribou Park by way of a 60-day "welcome to retirement" trip. Scott Warner photo

we were as vulnerable as the leaves of the trembling aspens around us.

Regardless of what brings you here, you will surely run out of time before you run out of destinations, but the seven-day loop we propose will give you a good introduction to the park, provide some lush scenery, take you past some pictograph sites, bear witness to the fire and re-growth cycle, and allow you to test your angling skills on some very cooperative walleye, northern pike and lake trout. This trip plan has no overly long portages and includes a couple of short days if you need a rest or get caught in bad weather.

You start by being shuttled to Leano Lake by Albert Rogalinski of Goldseekers Outfitting in Red Lake. It's possible to drive there on your own, but not worth the hassle. The road is poorly maintained, and use of Albert's services is highly recommended.

Since conditions within the park can change with each season and each passing storm, you'll want to stay informed, and a call to the park staff or Albert is advised. Albert is the main outfitter in the park and keeps current with conditions through debriefing his clients and liaising with the park staff; he's an ideal resource.

Your route will take you northwest to Jake and Mexican Hat Lakes, then through Glenn and Hansen Lakes on the way to Wrist Lake. Next you'll travel through Jigsaw, Haven and Adventure before turning south to Welkin and South

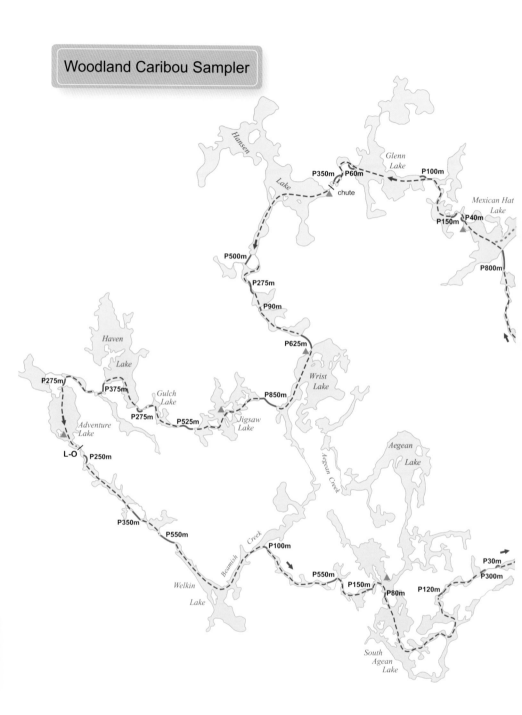

Woodland Caribou Sampler

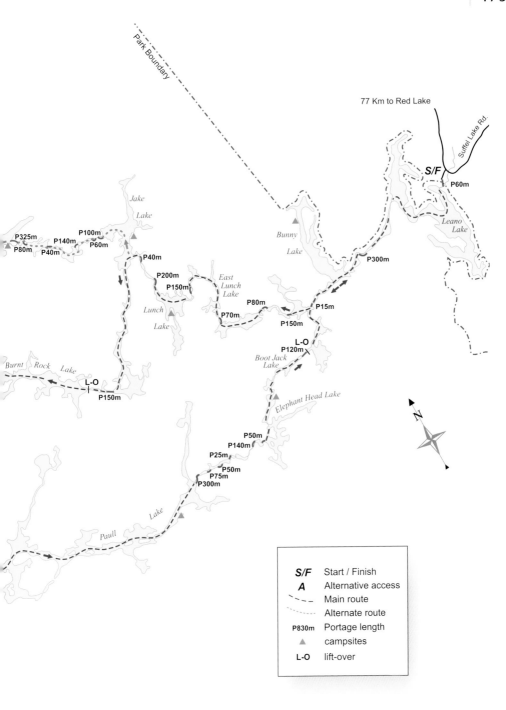

Park Boundary

77 Km to Red Lake

Suffel Lake Rd.

S/F

P60m

Leano Lake

Jake Lake

P325m
P140m
P100m
P80m
P40m
P60m

P40m

Bunny Lake

P300m

P200m
P150m

East Lunch Lake

Lunch Lake

P80m
P70m
P150m

P15m

L-O
P120m

Boot Jack Lake

Burnt Rock Lake

L-O
P150m

Elephant Head Lake

P50m
P140m
P25m
P50m
P75m
P300m

N

Paull Lake

S/F	Start / Finish
A	Alternative access
– – –	Main route
·········	Alternate route
P830m	Portage length
▲	campsites
L-O	lift-over

0 1 2 3 4km

Moose cow and calf at Barclay Lake. Scott Warner photo

Aegean. From here, head east to Elephant Head and Boot Jack to complete the seven-day loop. There are alternatives if you find yourself short of time or energy. Just remember to get the park map and to transcribe all the portages onto your set of topographical maps. As always, take your time and travel quietly, you never know what's just around the next bend. Keep your camera available as you travel; you'll find lots of suitable subjects.

Day one will end at Jake Lake and be fairly easy with seven portages and three liftovers. Paddle north on Leano to the outlet and a possible liftover. We floated through, but I've heard that there's a beaver dam there now. Further west, you'll come to a 60-rod (328 yd/300 m) portage on the left. The path is well worn, and it's good to know that you've got the longest portage of the day behind you. Crossing the south end of Bunny Lake brings you to a 3-rod (16 yd/15 m) portage on the right, followed in fairly quick succession by portages of 30 and 15 rods (164 and 87 yd/150 and 80 m). After the second of these, keep your eyes open for pitcher plants along the north shore.

Soon after is East Lunch Lake, reached by way of a 15-rod (76 yd/70 m) portage and a liftover. Paddle northeast and then west to get to the outlet, and do the 30-rod (164 yd/150 m) portage on the right to Lunch Lake. Look for more pitcher plants as you pass through the narrow section before the lake.

Now that you're on Lunch Lake, realize why it's called that and stop for a bite. There's a nice spot just as you enter the lake on a point on the south side. This is also a good spot for a swim. You can take your time here because you've only got a couple of miles and two portages before you get to Jake Lake. After lunch, head to the north end of Lunch Lake and the 40-rod (218 yd/200 m) portage on the right. The next half hour of paddling contains a liftover and your last portage of the day, an 8-rod (44 yd/40 m) carry on the right. Turn north on Jake Lake to the narrows, where there's a nice campsite on the right. Settle in, brew up a pot of coffee or tea, go for a swim, and then get out those red and white spoons and troll some of the bays for northern pike. Rest easy tonight because tomorrow will also be a light day, with the promise of some good walleye fishing to end the day.

Day two's destination is Mexican Hat Lake, with two possible routes: the short route out of the northwest corner of Jake, and the longer route to the southwest and through Burnt Rock Lake. If the wind is strong out of the northwest, then take the shorter route, otherwise take the scenic route through Burnt Rock. There are fewer portages and you'll enjoy the rugged beauty of Burnt Rock. Don't worry about the 160-rod (875 yd/800 m) portage at the end of the day — it's easy. Personally, I'd rather do one longer portage than five short ones. Paddle southwest on Jake Lake to the 30-rod (164 yd/150 m) portage, then a short hop to a liftover. After this you've got 2.5 miles (4 km) of paddling to enjoy Burnt Rock before encountering an easy 12-rod (65 yd/60 m) carry.

Two miles (3 km) later and you're at the 160-rod (875 yd/800 m) portage that will take you to Mexican Hat. It starts out on level ground, crosses the stream, and then descends into Mexican Hat. If you want to take advantage of the fishing, paddle east and camp near the waterfall entering the lake. The walleye fishing is usually good here. Lake trout fishing can also be productive on Mexican Hat. If fishing is not your thing, then head north and camp on the west shore as the lake narrows. The site here is large and offers good shelter as well as a great spot to swim. From this site you can also visit the sandbar just to the north to see the tracks of its latest visitors.

Tomorrow will be a little more strenuous, so relax and enjoy your evening. Locate your tobacco if you haven't left any offerings yet, as you'll have the opportunity to view two pictograph sites.

Day three's travel will encompass Glenn and Hansen Lakes on the way to Wrist Lake. At the north end of Mexican Hat there are two portages of 8 and 30 rods (44 and 164 yd/40 and 150 m), both on the left, a mile-and-half (2 km) paddle north and a 10-rod (109 yd/100 m) portage on the right leads to Glenn Lake. Cross Glenn in a northwesterly direction to its outlet and do the 12-rod (65 yd/60 m) portage on the left. A short distance downstream and a 70-rod 382 yd/350 m) portage on the right is necessary. This can be done as two short hops of 27 rods (147 yd/135 m) on the right, float across the pool, and 6 rods (33 yd/30 m) on the left, but the 70-rod (382 yd/350 m) is quicker. The next obstacle is defined on the park map as a chute. For us, this brings visions of something that should be approached with caution and definitely not run with a loaded canoe. This one could best be described as a micro-chute. For most, it will be an 8-rod (44 yd/40 m) carry on the right. In higher water, this is a Class I rapid has about a two-foot drop and can be run by starting on the left and holding to the center. There can be a strong current, so scout it first, and if in doubt, remember that it's only an 8-rod (44 yd/40 m) portage.

Hansen Lake contains two pictograph sites, one at the north end near the outlet and one to the southwest on the way to the 100-rod (546 yd/500 m) portage leading toward Wrist Lake. If the water on Hansen is high, you might try the stream to the south, but by midsummer the portage will be necessary.

It was at this second pictograph site that Kathy asked the spirit of the shaman to give us an indication that he was present. Leaving the pictograph, we approached the next portage, where we encountered an immature eagle sitting on a blowdown. We approached to within about 50 feet (15 m) as Kathy talked to it and I asked for permission to take its picture. It perched quietly, providing a great photo-op, then flew straight back to the pictograph site.

After the 100-rod (546 yd/500 m) portage you'll cross a small lake. The portage out of here requires you to penetrate the marsh on the south and work your way up a small stream to find the carry that starts on the left and then crosses the stream before depositing you in another small lake after 55 rods (300 yd/275 m). It took us over an hour to find this portage since the water was low, so just persevere here.

A short paddle and another 16-rod (87 yd/80 m) portage leaves you just one lake short of Wrist. Paddle half an hour south to the 125-rod (684 yd/625 m) carry into Wrist. As you come out to Wrist Lake, the forest thins out and there is a beautiful campsite just west of here on the north shore. This is one of the places where a caribou came to visit us (if you are up for it, Wrist has both lake trout and pike).

I had asked the spirits to teach me any lessons that they thought would be of benefit — again with remarkable results. Leaving Wrist Lake was an interesting humility day, a real lesson from the Great Spirit about handling adversity. We got our usual start and were on the water around 7:45 A.M., and we got our gear across the 170-rod (930 yd/850 m) portage to Haven. But when I returned for the canoe, I noticed that our sprout bag was missing from its appointed place, hanging from beneath the bow seat. You know that sinking feeling? How could I be so stupid as to not put them where they belong? I remember setting them out on a rock in preparation for getting the canoe in the water, but obviously they were not placed in the canoe. I had high hopes that we'd be able to do more distance than planned today, but that was now dashed. I was in a real snit.

We had to return to our campsite for the sprouts. They were not damaged, but my ego and energy level sure were. I spent so much energy being angry that by mid-afternoon I was exhausted. An interesting thing, though: as we were leaving the campsite that morning, I was humming the Rolling Stones' tune "You can't always get what you want but if you try sometimes you just might find you get what you need."

Day four was a little easier after yesterday's longer journey. Only five portages today as you make your way to Adventure Lake. Follow the north shore of Wrist to the 170-rod (930 yd/850 m) carry in to Jigsaw Lake. The portage ended in a floating bog when we were there, so be prepared for the sensation that you're walking on a water bed, only your ankles might get wet. Once you are on the water, you'll get the significance of its name. It takes some careful map and compass work to successfully traverse to the west end and the 105-rod (574 yd/525 m) portage to Haven Lake. Cross a small lake by traveling northwest and do the 55-rod (300 yd/275 m) carry to Haven Lake. Haven contains a good population of walleye and northern pike if you want to try your luck.

A third of the way up Haven on the west side, there's a bay that contains the 75-rod (410 yd/375 m) portage to Adventure. A half-hour paddle north brings you to the final carry of the day, a 55-rod (300 yd/275 m) to Adventure Lake. Your campsite is on the southern point of the large island at the south end of the lake. It's an elevated site with a nice cliff for diving and swimming. If you've got the time and the inclination, try fishing for lake trout, but watch out for those hungry pike.

On day five you are headed to South Aegean and will camp very near the pictograph site there. Begin by going south to a liftover and a 50-rod (273 yd/250 m) portage out of Adventure. About two miles (3 km) to the south is a 70-rod (382 yd/350 m) portage that is noted on the park map as "wet." If your boots aren't wet yet, they will be.

Nothing worse than a crazed grouse blocking the portage. Scott Warner photo

The next portage, a 110-rod (600 yd/550 m) affair will lead you to Welkin Lake. Paddle to the central portion of the lake and turn east for about 2 miles (3 km) to find a 20-rod (109 yd/100 m) portage to a narrow unnamed lake. This portage is easy and sets you up for the 110-rod (600 yd/550 m) portage to the south and will probably get your boots full

Are we there yet? Kathy Warner photo

again, as it has some "damp" sections. Stop for lunch along this small lake to rest and dry out your socks.

A 30-rod (164 yd/150 m) portage into Aegean, followed by a 16-rod (87 yd/80 m) carry just around the corner into South Aegean, will end your carrying for the day. Travel south and then east toward Paull Lake. There are campsites at the end of the long peninsula on both sides of the narrows. Be sure to visit the pictograph here and thank the spirits for getting you through the day.

There are lake trout here just waiting for your lure to drift by. Tomorrow will take you through Paull, a long east-west lake, so I'd suggest getting an early start if the breezes have been from the east.

Day six. We'll start with three portages of 24, 60 and 6 rods (130, 328 and 32 yd/120, 300 and 30 m) to get to Paull Lake. Now there's about a 7.5-mile (12 km) paddle to the east end and the 60-rod (328 yd/300 m) portage to Elephant Head. With no wind or with a breeze from the west, this is a very enjoyable leg. Get out the trout rigs if the spirit strikes you and the breeze is from the west. When the lake turns northeast you'll find the portage in a small bay on the east side.

Over the next 2.5 miles (4 km) there are six portages and a liftover, so have some lunch or a snack here and get hydrated. It's not that the portages are long, it's just that they follow one another in close succession. The six portages are 60, 15, 10, 5, 28 and 10 rods (328, 82, 55, 27, 153 and 55 yd/300, 75, 50, 25, 140 and 50 m). At least they're all fairly short and in no time you'll be turning north to the liftover in to Boot Jack. A little over half mile away there are points on both the north and south shores. There are campsites here. Kick back, have that libation and enjoy your evening. Eat the last of your snack food because tomorrow you can get more in Red Lake.

Day seven is another short one, with only a 24-rod (131 yd/120 m) portage and a liftover to get to the point where you turn east and repeat the 3 rods (16 yd z/15 m) to Bunny Lake, the 60 rods (328 yd/300 m) and liftover to Leano. If you are up early, you can have lunch at the landing while you are waiting for your ride back to Red Lake.

Please remember that routes and portages here are subject to changing conditions due to natural forces, so be ready for some obstacles. That's why I recommend checking with Albert both during your planning stage and just before your trip.

Woodland Caribou Sampler Route

LENGTH: 7–8 days

PORTAGES: 42

LONGEST PORTAGE: 170 rods
(875 yd/800 m)

DIFFICULTY: Intermediate canoe-tripping skills are required due to the remoteness of the route.

ACCESS: The Leano Lake access is located 77 km WSW from Red Lake. Travel Highway 618 west toward the town of Madsen for approximately 6 miles (10 km) from the traffic lights in Red Lake (hey, it's a small town and there is only one set of lights). Stay on the 618 and go beyond the town of Madsen, prepare to turn north off the paved road and onto Flat Lake Road. After approximately half a mile, Flat Lake veers to the west and becomes known as Suffle Lake Forest Access Road. Stay on this road and follow the parks signs to the Mile 51 turn off. At Mile 51 turn west and proceed approximately 3 miles (5 km) to the Leano Lake parking area. An alternative gravel road access of 68 miles (110 km) in length can be found by traveling west from the town of Ear Falls along Manitou Falls Road, north along Iriam Lake Road, then west at Mile 51 Road to the Leano Lake access point.

PERMITS: Advance permit reservations are currently not required and permits are available at the Woodland Caribou Provincial Park Office located at 227 Howey Street in Red Lake, or at Goldseekers Canoe Outfitting located in Red Lake at 75 Forestry Rd.

Special Note: due to a fire in 2006 the MNR Building at 227 Howey St., the Park Office has been temporarily re-located to the MNR Fire Base located at end of Forestry Rd. A self-serve kiosk has also been set up at the Red Lake Museum located on the west side of Highway 105.

ALTERNATIVE ACCESS: None

TOPOGRAPHICAL MAPS:
52L/15 Rostoul Lake 52L/16
Medicine Stone Lake

Quetico is truly a paddler's paradise.

Before You Go

THERE ARE SOME LOGISTICS INVOLVED in paddling Quetico Provincial Park. Some are simple and some are complex. It's important to note, however, that some planning is definitely required before you go.

Reservations

Make a reservation. Obtaining a permit on the day you arrive is possible, but getting one for the busier access points will be next to impossible.

Reservations can be made up to five months in advance.

You can phone for a reservation. Call 1-888-ONT-PARK (668-7275), or 519-826-5290 for outside of North America, and have the following information available before you call:

◆ park name
◆ arrival/departure dates
◆ access point # and or name (#21 Batchewung Lake)
◆ your name, address, postal code and telephone number and email address (if available)
◆ number in the party
◆ method of payment (e.g. credit card number, cheque or money order)

Changing or canceling a reservation:

Changes or cancellations in your reservation can be made by phoning 1-888-ONT-PARK (668-7275).

The reservation fee is non-refundable. You have 72 hours prior to your departure date to cancel without paying any penalties.

General Information

Quetico Provincial Park
108 Saturn Avenue
Atikokan, Ontario
807-597-2735
www.ontarioparks.com

Friends of Quetico
PO Box 1959
Atikokan, Ontario
P0T 1C0
807-929-2571
www.friendsofquetico.com

Quetico Foundation
48 Young St., Suit 610
Toronto, Ontario
M5E 1G6
416-941-9388
www.queticofoundation.org

Obtaining a Park Permit

◆ You must have a valid park permit to enter the interior of Quetico Provincial Park.

◆ Permits are picked up and fees are paid at one of the six designated ranger stations (Issuing Stations).

◆ Each ranger station is staffed by park employees.

◆ After picking up your permit you must then begin your interior trip by way of one of the 20 official Entry Points (take note that some of these points aren't actually starting points but simply lakes or rivers you must paddle through at the start of your trip).

Ranger Stations (and Neighboring Entry Points)

Dawson Trail Ranger Station (main campground) for entry points:
11-Baptism Lake and 12-Pickerel Lake

Directions: Located at the main campground in the northeast corner of the park, just south off Highway 11. It's a 130-mile (210 km) drive west of Thunder Bay and 24 miles (39 km) east of Atikokan.

Alternative: Stanton Bay, located about three-quarters of the way down Pickerel Lake, is used to avoid the long paddle across French and Pickerel Lakes. Permits must first be picked up at Dawson Trail Ranger Station. Then drive west on Highway 11 for 6.5 miles (10 km), a half-mile (1 km) past the intersection of Highway 11 and 633. It's a very rough gravel road that takes approximately 40 minutes to reach the small parking area. From here you have to portage 90 rods (492 yd/450 m) to the lake. The portage is located just to the right of the upper right-hand corner of the parking lot. At this point only Canadian paddlers can legally park overnight here. If you are a non-resident you must use a Canadian Outfitter to drop you off there. (I'm just as confused about this one as you are.)

Atikokan Ranger Station (park headquarters) for the central north entry points: 21-Batchewaung Lake, 22-Sue Falls and 23 Mack Lake

Directions: The park headquarters are located in the town of Atikokan. Drive north on Highway 11B, off Highway 11. The headquarters are on the right as you enter the town.

Alternative: Lerome Lake is not in the park boundary but can be used, after a day's paddling and portaging through a chain of small lakes, to reach the 22-Sue Falls entry point. To reach it, drive only 5.5 miles (9 km) west of Atikokan, south of Highway 11. A quarter-mile dirt road leads down to the lake. Parking is limited, however, and I strongly recommend you have one of the outfitters in Atikokan take you there.

Beaverhouse Lake Ranger Station for entry points: 31 Cirrus Lake and 32 Quetico Lake.

Directions: From Atikokan drive west on Highway 11 for 24 miles (39 km) then turn south on the dirt road opposite of Flanders Road (look for the park sign). It's 14 miles (22 km) to the parking area. The road is gravel but well maintained until where it forks at the 9-mile (15 km) mark. Take the left fork. The remaining way is rough and a much smaller roadway. Make sure you contact the park prior to your trip and ask about conditions. From the parking area you have to portage straight south for 120 rods (656 yd/600 m) to reach the lake. The ranger station is situated in a small, deep southeast bay of Beaverhouse Lake

Lac la Croix Ranger Station for entry points: 41-Threemile Lake, 42-Maligne River, 43-McAree Lake and 44-Bottle Lake (Crooked Lake)

Directions: To reach the Native Reserve and ranger station of Lac la Croix continue past the second fork on the Beaverhouse Lake access road. The total distance once you turn south off Highway 11 is 50 miles (79 km). This is a rough, seasonally maintained road, so make sure to phone the park prior to your trip to ask about conditions. Parking and a canoe launch are available in the small town of Lac la Croix, and the ranger station is located in a small bay along the north shore, about a half-an-hour paddle from town.

Prairie Portage Ranger Station for entry points: 51-Basswood River, 52-Sarah Lake, 53-Kashapiwi Lake, 61-Agnes Lake and 62-Carp Lake

Directions: Prairie Portage Ranger Station is reached by paddling north on Moose, Newfound and Sucker Lakes and then portaging 28 rods (153 yd/140 m) over to Basswood Lake. The cabin is to your right. But before that, you must drive northeast out of Ely, Minnesota. Take Highway 169 (Fernberg Road) and then Moose Lake Road. It's 19 miles (31 km) from Ely to the public launch.

Cache Bay Ranger Station for entry points: 71-Knife Lake, 72-Man Chain, 73-Falls Chain and 74-Boundary Point

Directions: The ranger station is located in Saganaga Lake's Cache Bay, on a small island not too far from the mouth of the bay. The majority of Saganaga Lake is American owned where motors not exceeding 25 horsepower are allowed. No motors are allowed on the Canadian side. To reach the public launch on the most southern inlet of Saganaga Lake take the 56-mile (90 km) Cook County Lake Road (Gunflint Trail Road) to its very northwestern end. The road begins in the town of Grand Marais, Minnesota.

Where Are the Portage and Campsites Signs?

In keeping with Quetico's "wilderness concept" philosophy, the portage take-outs are not marked with the commonly used bright-yellow portage signs. The location of a portage is shown on the park map, but none of the trails themselves are marked. The same rule applies to campsites, as well, except the map doesn't even indicate their whereabouts. With this in mind, you can camp anywhere within the boundaries of the park as long as you practice low-impact camping. If that doesn't match your style of tripping, then check out W.A. Fisher Maps or McKenzie Maps for Quetico; both have the major campsites marked.

Remote Border Crossing

With portions of Quetico Provincial Park situated along the border of Canada and the United States, some routes will begin and/or end in either country. That's where the Remote Area Border Crossing (RABC) permit comes in. It allows you to cross the border into Canada at certain "remote" areas without reporting to a port of entry. Canadian citizens and permanent residents of the U.S. can apply. There's a fee ($30 Canadian in 2006). You can apply in person to an Immigration Officer at any regular border crossing (i.e., Pigeon River, Rainy River, Fort Frances, Emerson) or by mail:

Canada Immigration Centre
Suite 108, 221 Archibald Street North, Thunder Bay Ontario P7C 3Y3
(807) 624-2158
or download an application at:
www.queticopark.com/rabc/index.html

Maps

Quetico Provincial Park and Friends of Quetico, in association with Chrismar Mapping Service, has produced an excellent park map for traveling in the interior.

Canadian Topographic Maps

W. A. Fisher Maps **www.fishermaps.com**

McKenzie Maps **www.bwcamaps.com**

Etopo – digital maps for Quetico **http://etopo.maps.ca**

Fish Species

Quetico lakes are home to five main sport fish: walleye (W), Northern Pike (NP), Smallmouth Bass (B), Largemouth Bass (LB), and Lake Trout (LT). The following list shows the fish species in each Quetico Lake listed in the routes described (not all lakes are listed).

Agnes Lake – W, NP, B, LT

Alice Lake – NP

Argo Lake – NP, LT

Badwater Lake – W, NP, LT

Baptism Lake – NP

Basswood – W, NP, B, LT

Batchewaung Bay – W, NP, LT

Beaverhouse Lake –
   W, NP, B, LT

Bentpine Lake – W, NP

Brent Lake – W, NP, LB, LT

Buckingham Lake – W, NP, LT

Burke Lake – W, NP, B, LB, LT

Cahe Bay – NP, LT

Cache Lake – W, NP, B, LT

Chatterton Lake – W, NP

Crooked Lake – W, NP, B, LT

Darkwater Lake – W, NP, B, LT

Elizabeth Lake – W, NP

Fern Lake – W, NP

French Lake – W, NP, LT

Glacier Lake – W, B, LT

Heronshaw Lake – W, NP

Howard Lake – NP

Isabela Lake – W, NP, B, LB

Jack Lake – W, NP

Jean Lake – W, NP, B, LB

Jesse Lake – W, NP

Kahshahpiwi Lake –
   W, NP, B, LT

Kawnipi Lake — W, NP,

Keats Lake – W, NP

Keefer Lake – W, NP, LT

Little Pine Lake – NP

Louisa Lake – NP, LT

Make Lake – W, NP, LB

McAlpine Lake – W, LT

McDougal Lake – NP, LT

McEwen Lake – W, NP, B, LT

McIntyre Lake – W, NP, LT

McNiece Lake – NP, LT

Olifaunt Lake – W, NP, B, LT

Oriana Lake – W, NP, LB, LT

Pickerel Lake – W, NP, B, LT

Poohbah Lake – W, NP, B, LT

Quetico Lake –
   W, NP, B, LB, LT

Rawn Lake – W, NP, LT

Roland Lake – W, NP, LT

Russell Lake – W, NP

Saganaga Lake – W, NP, LT

Saganagons Lake – W, NP, LT

Sarah Lake – W, NP, B, LB, LT

Shade Lake – W, NP, B, LB, LT

Shelley Lake – W, NP

Silence Lake – W, NP, B, LB, LT

Sturgeon Lake – W, NP, B,

Sunday Lake – W, LP, B, LB, LT

Tanner Lake – W, NP

Trant Lake – LB

Trousers Lake – NP

Walter Lake – W, NP, B, LT

Wawiag River – W

Your Lake – W, NP,

Yum Yum Lake – W, NP, B, LT

It's amazing to think that canoe traffic in Quetico is less busy now than during the fur-trade years.

Outfitters

Northern Access (Canada)

Seine River Lodge and Outfitters
PO Box 546
Atikokan, ON
P0T 1C0
1-807-947-2391 (summer) or
905-377-9736 (winter)
www.seineriverlodge.on.ca

Canadian Quetico Outfitters
1184 Mountain Road
Thunder Bay, ON
P7J 1C2
1-807-929-2177 (summer) or
1-807-475-3786 (winter)
www.canoecountry.com/cqo

Wyteki Outfitters
PO Box 546
Atikokan, Ontario
P0T 1C0
807-947-2391
www.quetico-canoe-trips.com

QuetiQuest Outfitters
PO Box 1060
Atikokan, Ontario
P0T 1C0
807-929-2266
www.quetiquest.com

Southern Access (United States)

Boundary Waters Canoe Trip Adventures
2700 Echo Trail
PO Box 327
Ely, MN 55731
1-800-510-2947
www.boundarywaterscanoetrips.com

Boundary Waters Outfitters &
    Timber Trail Resort
629 Kawishiwi Trail
Ely, Minnesota 55731
218-365-4879 or 1-800-777-7348
www.boundarywatersoutfitters.com

Canadian Border Outfitters
14635 Canadian Border Road
Ely, MN 55731
1-800-247-7530
www.canoetrip.com

Canadian Waters Outfitters
111 East Sheridan Street
Ely, MN 55731-1299
1-800-255-2922
www.canadianwaters.com

Canoe Country Outfitters
629 East Sheridan Street
PO Box 30
Ely, MN 55731
1-800-752-2306 or 1-218-365-4046
www.canoecountryoutfitters.com

Jordan's Canoe Outfitters
& Wilderness Shop
1701 Highway 1
Ely, MN 55731
1-800-644-9955 or 1-218-365-8129
www.jordans-outfitters.com

La Tourell's Moose Lake Outfitters
PO Box 239
Ely, MN 55731
1-800-365-4531
www.latourells.com

Moose Track Adventures
593 Kawishiwi Trail
Ely, MN 55731
1-800-777-7091 or 1-218-365-4106
www.moosetrackadventures.com

River Point Outfitting Company
PO Box 397
Ely, MN 5580
1-800-456-5580
www.elyoutfitters.com

Voyageur North Outfitters
1829 E Sheridan Street
Ely, MN 55731-1948
1-800-848-5530 or 218-365-3251
www.vnorth.com

Wilderness Outfitters
1 E Camp Street
Ely, MN 55731
1-800-777 8572 or 218-365-3211
www.wildernessoutfitters.com

Southeast Corner (United States)

Clearwater Canoe Outfitters and Lodge
on the Gunflint Trail
774 Clearwater Rd.
Grand Marais, MN   55604
1-800-527-0554 or 218-388-2254
www.clearwateroutfitters.com

Golden Eagle Lodge
Nordic Ski Center
468 Clearwater Road
Grand Marais, MN, 55604
1-800-346-2203 or 218-388-2203
www.golden-eagle.com

Gunflint Northwoods Outfitters
143 South Gunflint Lake
Grand Marais, MN 55604
1-800-328-3325 or 218-388-2294
www.gunflintoutfitters.com

Hungry Jack Outfitters
318 S. Hungry Jack Rd.
Grand Marais, MN 55604
1-800-648-2922
www.hjo.com

Rockwood Lodge and Canoe Outfitters
Gunflint Trail
50 Rockwood Road
Grand Marais, MN 55604
1-800-942-2922 or 218-388-2242
www.canoeoutfitter.com

Seagull Canoe Outfitters
12208 Gunflint Trail
Grand Marais, MN 55604
218-388-2216
www.seagulloutfitters.com

Superior North Outfitters
84 Sag Lake Trail
Grand Marais, MN 55604
1-800-852-2008 or 218-388-4416
www.superiornorthoutfitters.com/home.htm

Tuscarora Lodge and Outfitters
193 Round Lake
Grand Marais, MN 55604
1-800-544-3843 or 218-388-2221
www.tuscaroracanoe.com

Voyageur Canoe Outfitters
189 Sag Lake Trail
Grand Marais, MN 55604
1-888-CANOEIT or 218-388-2224
www.canoeit.com

Sawtooth Outfitters
7213 Hwy 61
PO Box 2214
Tofte, MN 55615
218-663-7643
www.sawtoothoutfitters.com

Sawbill Canoe Outfitters
4620 Sawbill Trail
Box 2129
Tofte, MN 55615
218-663-7150
www.sawbill.com

Southwest Corner (United States)

Anderson's Canoe Outfitters
7255 Crane Lake Road
Crane Lake, MN
55725
218-993-2287
www.anderson-outfitters.com

Gateway Resort and Outfitters
7614 Gold Coast Road
Crane Lake, MN 55725
218-993-2415
www.gatewayresort.net

La Croix Outfitters
5713 Crane Lake Road
Buyck, MN 55771
218-993-2642
www.lacroixoutfitters.com

Zups Outfitters
HC3 Box 80
Crane Lake, MN 55725
807-485-2492
www.zupsresort.com

Outfitters for White Otter Lake Route

Dream Catcher Tours
Shuttle Service and Boat Tours
Dennis Smyk
153 Balsam Street
PO Box 989
Ignace, Ontario
P0T 1T0
807-934-6482

Brown's Clearwater West Lodge
PO Box 1766
Dep't. I
Atikokan, Ontario
P0T 1C0
807-597-2884
www.brownsclearwaterlodge.com

Canoe Canada Outfitters
PO Box 1810
Atikokan, Ontario
P0T 1C0
807-597-6418
www.canoecanada.com

QuetiQuest Outfitters
PO Box 1060
Atikokan, Ontario
P0T 1C0
807-929-2266
www.quetiquest.com

Wyteki Outfitters
PO Box 546
Atikokan, Ontario
P0T 1C0
807-947-2391
www.quetico-canoe-trips.com

Agimak Lake Resort
PO Box 188
Ignace, Ontario
P0T 1T0
807-934-2891
www.agimaklake.com

For More Information:

Turtle River Provincial Park
PO Box 730
Dryden, Ontario
P8N 2Z4
807-223-7535
www.ontarioparks.com

Outfitters for Wabakimi

Huron Air and Outfitters
PO Box 122
Armstong, Ontario
P0T 1A0
807-583-2051
www.huronair.com

Mattice Lake Outfitters and Air Service
PO Box 157
Armstrong, Ontario
P0T 1A0
807-583-2483
www.matticelake.com

Wilderness Nature Tours
    and Expeditions Ltd.
R.R. #14 Dog Lake Road,
Thunder Bay, Ontario
P7B 5E5
807-767-2022
www.wabakimi.com/wildwaters
or
Frontier Trail, Hwy. 527
Armstrong, Ontario
P0T 1A0
807-583-2626

Smoothrock Camps
PO Box 278
Armstrong, Ontario   P0T 1A0
807-583-2617
www.smoothrock.com

Wilderness Connections
Attn: Jim Pearson
Armstrong, Ontario   P0T 1A0
807-583-1888 (summer)
519-371-1416 (winter)
www.wildernessconnections.ca

Via Rail Canada
1-888-VIARAIL (1-888-842-7245)
www.viarail.ca

For More Information:

Wabakimi Provincial Park / Ontario Parks
435 James St. S.
Suite 221d
Thunder Bay, Ontario   P7E 6S8
807-475-1634
www.wabakimi.on.ca/wabakimi

Outfitters for Albany River

Canoe Frontier Outfitters
PO Box 38
Pickle Lake, Ontario
P0V 3A0
866-285-8618
www.canoefrontier.com

For More Information:

Albany River Provincial Park
PO Box 970
Nipigon, Ontario
807-825-3403
www.ontarioparks.com

Outfitters for Woodland Caribou

Goldseekers Canoe Outfitting
& Wilderness Expeditions
PO Box 1152
Red Lake Ontario
P0V 2M0
1 800-591-9282
www.goldseekers.net
and:
Woodland Caribou Outfitters
Red Lake Ontario
1-(807)-727-2353
www.woodlandoutfitters.com

For More Information:

Woodland Caribou Provincial Park
PO Box 5003
Red Lake, Ontario
P0V 2M0
807-727-1329
www.ontarioparks.com
Note: Woodland Caribou Provincial Park has a
canoe route map available

Scott and Kathy Warner's website
60 days in Woodland Caribou Provincial Park
www.woodland-cariboupark.com

Bibliography

Abell, Sam. *Refuge from Civilization*. National Geographic, December edition, 1978.
Backes, David. *A Wilderness Within: The Life of Sigurd F. Olson*. Minnesota: Minnesota Press, 1997.
Barr, Elinor. *White Otter Castle: The Legacy of Jimmy McQuat*. Thunder Bay:
    The Friends of White Otter Castle, 1984.
Beymer, Robert. *A Paddler's Guide to Quetico Provincial Park*. Minnesota: W.A. Fisher Company, 1985.
Bolz, Arnold J. *Portage into the Past*. Minnesota: Minnesota Press, 1960.
Buck, Ken. *Bill Mason: Wilderness Artist from Heart to Hand*. Rocky Mountain Books, 2005.
Cummings, Dr. *Caribou Country*. Seasons, Summer edition, 1991.
Denis, K. *Canoe Trails Through Quetico*. Toronto: The Quetico Foundation, 1959.
Dewdney, Selwyn and Kenneth E. Kidd. *Indian Rock Paintings of the Great Lakes*. Toronto:
    University of Toronto Press, 1973.
Erickson, Bill. *Charlie's Guide to Lakes Paddled by Tier Scouts*. Northern Tier Scouts, 2006.
Furtman, Michael. *A Season for the Wilderness: The Journal of a Summer in Canoe Country*.
    Wisconsin: Northword Press Inc., 1989.
Furtman, Michael. *Magic on the Rocks*. Minnesota: Birch Portage Press, 2000.
Henderson, Bob. *The White Otter Castle*. Kanawa, Spring edition, 1998.
Huot–Vickery, Jim. *A Big Beloved Country*. Canoe Journal, 1999.
Labatt, Lori and Bruce Littlejohn. *Islands of Hope*. Toronto: Firefly Books, 1992.
Leopold, Aldo and Luna B. Leopold. *Round River*. New York: Oxford University Press, 1993.
Leopold, Aldo. *A Sand County Almanac: With Other Essays on Conservation from Round River*.
    New York: Oxford University Press, 1966.
Littlejohn, Bruce M. *Quetico–Superior Country*. Canadian Geographical Journal, 1965.
Lorbiecki, Marybeth. *Aldo Leopold: A Fierce Green Fire*. Helena, MT: Falcon Press, 1996.
Manzo, Helen Sue and Alesha Leanne Manzo. *Art Madsen's Snowshoe Baby*. Boundary Waters Journal,
    Winter edition, 2005.
Ministry of Natural Resources. *Lake Names of Quetico Provincial Park*. Atikokan, 1988.
Ministry of Natural Resources. *Pictographs of Quetico Provincial Park*. Atikokan, 1984.
Ministry of Natural Resources. *Turtle River Provincial Park Canoe Route Map*. Ignace, 1990.
Ministry of Natural Resources. *Turtle River Provincial Waterway Park Background
Information*. Ignace: 1990.
Morse, Eric. *Freshwater Saga*. Toronto: University of Toronto Press, 1987.
Morse, Eric. *Fur Trade Routes of Canada: Then and Now*. Toronto: University of Toronto Press, 1979.
Nute, Grace Lee. *The Voyageur's Highway*. Minnesota: Minnesota Historical Society, 1941, 2002.
Olson, Sigurd F. *Songs of the North*. Penguin Books, 1987, 1995.
Peake, Michael. *Tripping into Fall*. Che–Mun, Fall edition, 1993.
Peruniak, Shirley. *Quetico Provincial Park: An Illustrated History*. Atikokan: The Friends of Quetico, 2000.
Raffan, James. *Fire in the Bones: Bill Mason and the Canadian Canoeing Tradition*. Toronto:
    Harper Collins Publisher Ltd., 1996.
Reid, Ron. *The Trappers of Wabakimi Lake*. Seasons, Summer edition, 1981.
Rom, William N. M.D. *Canoe Country Wilderness*. Minnesota: Voyageur Press, 1987.
Solandt, Omand. *Sigurd Olson: Mister Voyageur*. Che–Mun, Summer edition, 1992.
Tanner, John. *The Falcon*. Penguin Books, 1830, 1994.
The Friends of Quetico. *Pages of the Past: Voyageurs and Early Explorers*. Atikokan, 1993.
The Friends of Quetico. *Quetico's Fascinating Facts*. Atikokan, 1998.
Searie, Newell R. *Saving Quetico–Superior: A Land Set Apart*. Minnesota:
    Minnesota Historical Society Press, 1977.
Unwin, Peter. *The Wolf's Head: Writing Lake Superior*. Toronto: Viking Canada, 2003.

www.ancientforest.org/guide.html
www.canoestories.com
www.eober.org
www.jon-nelson.com
www.myccr.com
www.queticopark.com
www.quetico-canoe-trips.com/canoeroutes.html
www.quietjourney.com/quetico/queticosurveyresults.html
www.quietjourney.com/stories/pdb/queticopark.html
www.rootbeerlady.com
www.seagulloutfitters.com/canoe_routes.html
www.woodlands-cariboupark.com

Index